American Railroad Labor
and the Genesis of the New Deal, 1919–1935

WORKING IN THE AMERICAS

UNIVERSITY PRESS OF FLORIDA

Florida A&M University, Tallahassee
Florida Atlantic University, Boca Raton
Florida Gulf Coast University, Ft. Myers
Florida International University, Miami
Florida State University, Tallahassee
New College of Florida, Sarasota
University of Central Florida, Orlando
University of Florida, Gainesville
University of North Florida, Jacksonville
University of South Florida, Tampa
University of West Florida, Pensacola

WORKING IN THE AMERICAS

Edited by Richard Greenwald, Drew University,
and Timothy Minchin, LaTrobe University

*Florida's Working-Class Past: Current Perspectives on Labor, Race, and Gender
from Spanish Florida to the New Immigration*, edited by Robert Cassanello
and Melanie Shell-Weiss (2008)

The New Economy and the Modern South, by Michael Dennis (2009)

Film Noir, American Workers, and Postwar Hollywood, by Dennis Broe (2009)

*Americanization in the States: Immigrant Social Welfare Policy, Citizenship, and National
Identity in the United States, 1908–1929*, by Christina A. Ziegler-McPherson (2009)

Black Labor Migration in Caribbean Guatemala, 1882–1923,
by Frederick Douglass Opie (2009)

Migration and the Transformation of the Southern Workplace since 1945,
edited by Robert Cassanello and Colin J. Davis (2010)

American Railroad Labor and the Genesis of the New Deal, 1919–1935,
by Jon R. Huibregtse (2010)

American Railroad Labor
and the Genesis of the New Deal,
1919–1935

Jon R. Huibregtse

FOREWORD BY RICHARD GREENWALD AND TIMOTHY MINCHIN

UNIVERSITY PRESS OF FLORIDA

Gainesville · Tallahassee · Tampa · Boca Raton

Pensacola · Orlando · Miami · Jacksonville · Ft. Myers · Sarasota

15 14 13 12 11 10   6 5 4 3 2 1

Library of Congress Cataloging-in-Publication Data
Huibregtse, Jon R.
American railroad labor and the genesis of the New Deal, 1919–1935 /
Jon R. Huibregtse ; foreword by Richard Greenwald and Timothy Minchin.
p. cm.—(Working in the Americas)
Includes bibliographical references and index.
ISBN 978-0-8130-3465-2 (alk. paper)
1. Railroads—Employees—Labor unions—United States—History—20th
century. 2. Railroads—United States—Employees—History—20th century.
3. Railroads—Employees—Legal status, laws, etc.—United States—
History—20th century. 4. Working class—United States—History—20th
century. 5. Working class—Political activity—United States—History—
20th century. 6. New Deal, 1933–1939. 7. United States—Economic
conditions—1918–1945. 8. United States—Social conditions—1918–1932.
9. United States—Politics and government—1919–1933. I. Title.
HD6515.R1H85 2010
331.88'11385097309042—dc22   2009040190

The University Press of Florida is the scholarly publishing agency for the
State University System of Florida, comprising Florida A&M University,
Florida Atlantic University, Florida Gulf Coast University, Florida
International University, Florida State University, New College of Florida,
University of Central Florida, University of Florida, University of North
Florida, University of South Florida, and University of West Florida.

University Press of Florida
15 Northwest 15th Street
Gainesville, FL 32611-2079
http://www.upf.com

To Jessica and Maggie

Contents

Illustrations

Foreword

The 1920s have long been described as "the Lean Years" for American workers. They followed the dynamism of the progressive era and World War I as workers and social reformers attempted to remake America. In the wake of this activism, the 1920s seemed like a retreat (either forced or voluntary) for labor. These were after all years filled with the Red Scare, open shop, welfare capitalism, Americanization, and what seemed like an all-out assault on labor unions. These were also the years of rising consumerism and the celebration of the individual over the collective. American workers seemed lulled into inactivity, from policy and political debates.

Jon Huibregtse reminds us that the surface can be deceiving. While it would be wrong to read the 1920s as only a precursor to the New Deal, scholars have been curious to locate the roots to modern liberalism for many years. Huibregtse joins this growing list, who see the 1920s as significant to understanding the shift from Progressivism to liberalism. He roots his story in the railroad industry and with its workers. Rail workers had a unique history. Their industry was heavily regulated and emerged from World War I as government run. They combined the quest for collective bargaining with citizen rights and industrial democracy, bridging to the New Deal. Building on the growing number of studies that have looked at the changing relationship between the state and workers, Huibregtse's great force has been his ability to place workers as central to this shift. He demonstrates clearly that workers affect policy, that they are active participants in policy debates, and that the experiences of rail workers proved important educational experiences for the New Deal.

RICHARD GREENWALD AND TIMOTHY MINCHIN
SERIES EDITORS

Acknowledgments

In the early stages of this project Daniel Nelson of the University of Akron offered advice and comments that helped me tremendously to clarify my argument, thinking, and prose. H. Roger Grant offered unfettered access to his personal collection of the *Brotherhood of Locomotive Engineers Journal*. Robert Gough and James Oberly at the University of Wisconsin-Eau Claire first encouraged me to study railroad workers. Library and archival staffs at the University of Akron, Kent State University, Cornell University, the Library of Congress, the Wisconsin State Historical Society, the University of Colorado, the College of the Holy Cross, the Ohio Historical Society, the Franklin D. Roosevelt Presidential Library, the Herbert C. Hoover Presidential Library, and Georgetown University were all ready to lend assistance when needed. Neal Conrad, the Framingham State College interlibrary loan specialist, also gave much-appreciated assistance. Richard Allen offered advice and support as I completed the manuscript. Much of the final writing occurred while I was on sabbatical, and I am thankful to the administration and Board of Trustees of Framingham State College for that opportunity. I must also thank Bruce Cohen, Robert Dykstra, Wythe Holt, Joseph McCartin, and Nicholas Racheotes, all of whom read all or part of the manuscript. I appreciated their comments and suggestions; the book is better because of their efforts. I owe a tremendous professional debt to P. Bradley Nutting; I hope this book is, in part, a testament to his good judgment. Robin Robinson, FSC's director of Academic Technology and Distance Education, provided last-minute, and much-appreciated, technical support. David Landgraf made several trips to the Wisconsin State Historical Society to copy material for me.

My greatest debt is to my family, especially my parents, Roland and Patricia Huibregtse, who are a source of inspiration. Ellen Zimmerman was encouraging and supportive as I completed this project. She read countless pages, and this book has fewer mistakes because of her critical eye. Her truly significant contribution, however, was to pull me away from professional demands and to create a home that is full of love. Finally, this book is dedicated to my daughters, Jessica and Maggie, who remind me daily of life's real treasures.

Abbreviations

AFL	American Federation of Labor
ARE	Association of Railway Executives
ATSF	Atchison, Topeka & Santa Fe Railroad
BLE	Brotherhood of Locomotive Engineers
BLFE	Brotherhood of Locomotive Firemen and Engineers
BRT	Brotherhood of Railroad Trainmen
BRSC	Brotherhood of Railway and Steamship Clerks, Freight Handlers, Express, and Station Employees
CPPA	Conference for Progressive Political Action
FOE	Fraternal Order of Eagles
ICC	Interstate Commerce Commission
NAM	National Association of Manufacturers
NBA	National Board of Mediation
NMB	National Mediation Board
ORC	Order of Railway Conductors
RED	American Federation of Labor–Railroad Employees Department
RENPA	Railroad Employees National Pension Association
RLA	Railway Labor Act
RLB	Railroad Labor Board
RLEA	Railroad Labor Executives Association
RRA	Railroad Retirement Act
SUNA	Switchmens Union of North America
T&NO	Texas and New Orleans Railroad
UMW	United Mine Workers
USRA	United States Railroad Administration

Introduction

According to David Montgomery, prior to World War I, the American Federation of Labor (AFL) defined the parameters of legitimate trade unionism.[1] The government crushed radicalism during and after the war, and the AFL lost the influence that it wielded during the Wilson administration. In the years between the end of World War I and the onset of the Great Depression, however, the independent railroad brotherhoods and their partners in the American Federation of Labor–Railroad Employees Department (RED) challenged and surpassed the main body of the AFL as the most articulate, active voices of American labor, and helped to shape the future relationship between the federal government and workers.

Organized railroad labor emerged from World War I both politically and financially stronger than it had been at any time in its history. By 1920 union ranks had swelled to five million, a 74 percent increase over the previous decade.[2] Railway workers contributed mightily to the war effort and they had obtained uniformity in work rules and conditions. These gains were largely due to the operating practices of the United States Railway Administration (USRA), which had controlled the carriers from late in 1917 to 1920. The necessity of keeping the trains operating was the government's primary motivation during the war and thus it was willing to grant concessions to labor.

Yet railway workers, along with the rest of organized labor, faced a crisis when the fighting ended because their wartime gains were in jeopardy. Railroaders feared that their advances would be lost when the USRA returned control of the carriers to management, which it was legally bound to do within twenty-one months of the end of the war. Congress faced a difficult question: how to return the carriers to private control and reconcile labor's desire to maintain its organizational advances with management's desire to assert full authority? Ellis W. Hawley notes that some historians have argued that an "organizational revolution" was under way by 1917 that was shifting power from old elites to financial institutions, corporate bureaucracies, and functional or occupational organizations.[3] In the railroad industry, labor unions fought with corporate elites to retain their recent gains. The government contributed to the organizational revolution by undertaking a greater role in managing a segment of the American economy.

The railroad unions used the language of industrial democracy popularized during the war to frame the debate to their members and the public. Joseph McCartin argues that industrial democracy was significant during World War I because it gave voice to workers' demands for organization in mass industries, which was also linked to the emerging regulatory potential of the federal government.[4] McCartin contends that after the post-war wave of strike defeats, labor did not turn again to the state again until the 1930s.[5] I disagree with McCartin on the latter point. I argue that the notions of industrial democracy did not die in the wave of post-war strikes, but were crucial to the brotherhoods' political efforts throughout the 1920s. The railroaders linked the need for workplace rights, such as collective bargaining, with their rights as American citizens. Many Americans viewed the war as much in terms of bringing democracy to themselves as to the citizens of Germany.[6] American workers lacked basic rights in their places of work, which violated the nation's democratic principles. The post-war union defeats bolstered their determination to assert their rights as American citizens through electoral political action.

The political efforts of railroad unions in the interwar years, especially up to 1935, illustrate the intensity of labor militancy in a period that historians have generally considered void of such activity. Railroaders were central figures in transforming pre-war Progressivism with its notions of "individualism" and industrial disorder and inefficiency[7] into twentieth-century liberalism. Industrial democracy was also central to this transformation, as was reliance on the state, although much of the new labor history has deemphasized the role of the state. Colin Davis argues that between 1912 and 1922 the state was a catalyst for shifting power relations between itself, labor, and capital that brought about a profound transformation in American society that affected workplaces, union halls, corporate offices, and political corridors of power.

He writes, "The state action played a critical role in this metamorphosis."[8] I argue that through political activities, the railroad unions prompted the state to remain a catalyst of change beyond 1922.

Steven Fraser argues that many people familiar with industrial relations recognized that the pre-war "Prussian method" of labor relations had to end and that "the financial and social costs of industrial discipline achieved through coercion were becoming exorbitant."[9] Workers in the railroad industry were uniquely positioned to effect the most change in the nation's political economy. Railroad unionists were not the only workers who sought to change the basic nature of employer-employee relations, but the federal government had long since established its authority to regulate labor relations in the industry through its power to regulate interstate commerce.[10]

Lizabeth Cohen, discussing the emergence of the New Deal labor policy a decade later, argues that while government support was an important aspect of the New Deal, it was still the enthusiasm and organizational spirit of workers themselves that made it a success.[11] This spirited enthusiasm had been present a decade earlier while the dynamics of the railroad industry and the political climate were much different in the 1920s. Writing of labor relations in the decade before the New Deal, Robert Zieger argues that the activities of railroad unionists forced both labor leaders and politicians to reevaluate their conception of the role of labor in politics.[12]

The railroad unions came together during the congressional debate in 1919–1920 over how to return the carriers to private control to form an alliance under the banner of the Plumb Plan League, which called for continued federal control of the carriers. The four independent brotherhoods that were not affiliated with the AFL—the Brotherhood of Locomotive Engineers (BLE), the Brotherhood of Locomotive Firemen and Enginemen (BLEF), the Brotherhood of Railroad Trainmen (BRT), and the Order of Railroad Conductors (ORC)—spearheaded the effort. The railroad unions affiliated with the AFL's Railroad Employees Department (RED) also worked closely with the independent brotherhoods, but the main body of the AFL remained distant. The Plumb Plan League was the first step in forging an important alliance between the unions, which had profound effects on American labor history. It is significant that unlike the AFL in the progressive era, the brotherhoods were able to sustain their political institutional base between congressional elections. The Plumb Plan League, its newspaper, *Labor*, and later the Railroad Labor Executive Association (RLEA) were all crucial in sustaining the political base.[13] Railroaders were joined in the League by many pre-war progressives, unionists, and socialists of various stripes.

The independent railroad brotherhoods and the RED became the most politically active segment of organized labor during the 1920s. The brotherhoods successfully applied political pressure to bring about the passage of the Railway Labor Act (RLA) of 1926 and amendments to it in 1934, and the Railroad Retirement Act (RRA) of 1935. These acts foreshadowed two significant pieces of New Deal social and labor legislation: the National Labor Relations Act and the Social Security Act. The unions adopted the AFL's political strategy of "electing friends and defeating enemies," but they were much more willing than the AFL to involve themselves in electoral politics in the post-war years.[14] This coalition also differed from the main body of the AFL by arguing for state intervention in order to secure labor's goals. Senator Robert Wagner, who was the principal author of the Social Security Act of 1935 and the Railroad Retirement Act, viewed the debate that surrounded the railroad legislation as a precursor to national social security.[15]

The wave of post-war strikes, the Red Scare, and the anti-labor climate of the 1920s have led historians to generally accept Irving Bernstein's interpretation of the decade of the 1920s as the "lean years" in American labor history.[16] Others have recognized the political efforts of the operating brotherhoods, but do not attach any long-term significance to them.[17]

Throughout the 1920s the railroad brotherhoods overshadowed the AFL in their vitality and efforts to gain advances for organized labor. Gwendolyn Mink argues that until the formation of the Congress of Industrial Organizations (CIO), the AFL spoke for the working class.[18] However, the American working class was large and diverse and the AFL represented only a minority of such workers, so to argue that the AFL spoke for the entire working class is risky. Although the railroad brotherhoods represented fewer workers than did the AFL, they promoted legislative solutions to long-standing labor problems, most importantly collective bargaining, that have affected American workers ever since. The Railway Labor Act of 1926, its 1934 Amendments, and the National Labor Relations Act all helped to reduce labor-management conflict through the agency of the state. President Woodrow Wilson's administration strengthened unions but failed to supplant labor-management conflict, which was the fundamental transition at which it aimed.[19]

The railroad unions helped to achieve what the Wilson administration failed to attain and thus contributed mightily to the evolution of the modern state. Using the ballot box, railroad unions created a centralized and rational bureaucratic system of managing labor relations in the industry in return for their own recognition.[20]

Labor historians often ignore the 1920s after unions suffered decisive defeats early in the decade, which largely eliminated wartime gains.[21] David Montgomery argues that "the decade after 1923 was a remarkable hiatus in the evolution of the labor movement."[22] By applying their concept of industrial democracy and linking it to such icons as Washington and Lincoln, the railroad unions actively sought to expand the workplace rights of their members through the electoral process.

Other scholars take a more politically centered approach. Melvyn Dubofsky argues that the federal government was in neutral concerning labor relations during the 1920s.[23] Ruth O'Brien, like Robert Zieger, recognizes the important relationship between the Republican Party and labor policy during the 1920s, but she makes the GOP the only actor at a time when organized labor, progressives of both parties, and the judiciary all helped to shape labor policy.[24]

The origins of New Deal labor policy were complex and the logical result of an evolutionary process that began late in the nineteenth century. The brotherhoods helped to shape New Deal policies, and further illustrated the grassroots nature of much of the New Deal.[25] The activities of the railroad brotherhoods were vital to the future of the American labor movement for several reasons. First, and perhaps most importantly, although railroad operatives gained the right to bargain collectively, they relied upon the good offices of the federal government to protect that right. When the federal government enacted the National Labor Relations Act in 1935, it extended collective bargaining protection to the rest of the American labor force, but made the federal government the enforcer and protector of those rights. As we have seen over the last three decades, organized labor, when federal support is withdrawn, has generally been unable to respond to employer initiatives to weaken organized labor. Secondly, the effort of railroad unions was essential to passage of the Social Security Act of 1935, which defined the federal government's central role in helping retirees or those who may have fallen on hard times. Finally, railroad workers articulated through the language of industrial democracy an idea of American industrial citizenship. Railroad labor, like many other American workers, asked rhetorically, "If we're fighting to bring democracy to Germany, why shouldn't we have it here too?" Although the rules of engagement had changed, in the 1920s railroad labor continued to fight "labor's great war."[26]

Historically, the independent railroad unions had remained outside the fray of partisan politics, and so their foray into the electoral process marked a significant watershed in their history. According to Joseph G. Rayback, the BLE lost a long, costly strike against the Michigan Southern and Indiana Railway in the 1860s and changed into a "moral uplift" society for the next half-century.[27] Their philosophy again took on a new form after World War I, however, and they subscribed to a notion of political economy that helped to philosophically bridge the early decades of the century and the New Deal.

In what follows, I argue that the united and well-organized union forces within the rail industry effectively moved within the precincts of American politics and that, as a result, they achieved legislative gains that transcended their own particular interests. Laurence Scott Zakson, writing in 1989, argued that while the role of federal courts' interpretation of the labor relations has been well documented, the history of labor relations legislation " . . . is still in its embryonic form."[28] By illustrating how workers themselves helped to shape labor policy, this work will help to fill some of the gap that Zakson identified.

The second chapter summarizes briefly the history of the railroad industry and its unions from the middle of the nineteenth century to the early twentieth century. The third chapter examines the industry during the Great War, the benefits the war brought railroaders, and the debate that surrounded the railroad industry as federal control drew to a conclusion in 1919. Congress enacted legislation and the railroad unions lost many of the prerogatives that they had gained during the period of federal oversight. The Esch-Cummins Bill, known officially as the Transportation Act of 1920, largely negated their wartime advances such as national agreements that established uniform work rules and pay scales. Unions mobilized for the election of 1920, and using the roll call vote on the Transportation Act as their guide, exhorted their members to vote. The railroad unions sustained a high level of political organization, which was the foundation of their political activism in the 1920s.

In the summer of 1922 approximately four hundred thousand railroad shopmen went on strike when wages were cut. The government crushed the strike and inspired the unions to even greater political activity. The midterm elections were clearly a setback for President Harding and the GOP, which saw its majority slip in Congress. Organized labor was quick to take credit for what it considered a major defeat for the "reactionaries."

The fourth chapter addresses the unions' actions between the midterm elections of 1922 and presidential election two years later. During this interval labor was busy pushing its version of a railroad labor relations bill, working closely with members of Congress and also the Association of Railroad Executives (ARE) to craft legislation that was acceptable to all parties. For the first time, labor was intimately involved in creation of statutes that would govern railroads. Although doomed from the beginning because of the hostility of the Republican congressional leadership and carrier opposition, the proposed Howell-Barkley Bill laid the foundation for what later became the Railway Labor Act. By the election of 1924, the railroad unions were moving away from their progressive allies, whom they had cultivated since 1920 and who generally favored a third political party, because they recognized that their best chance of influencing labor policy was to work within the mainstream of American politics.

Chapters 5 and 6 discuss the legislative struggles between the election of 1924 and passage of the Railway Labor Act in May 1926, which laid important legal framework for the National Labor Relations Act of 1935. Perhaps most significantly the RLA withstood a legal challenge when the Brotherhood of Railway and Steamship Clerks Union filed a suit against the Texas and New Orleans Railroad for attempting to stop union organization.

Chapter 7 examines the unions' efforts to amend the RLA, even though by the late 1920s some of the enthusiasm for political activism seemed to be waning. Nonetheless, by 1934 unions had played a significant role in amending the law, and in the process had firmly established the right of unions to exist, albeit with government support.

Chapter 8 examines the railroad unions' fight to create a railroad pension system, which was the legislative model of the Social Security Act. Passage of the Railroad Retirement Acts of 1934 and 1935 and the court challenges that they faced set important legal precedents, which helped insure that the Social Security Act would not be ruled unconstitutional. Senator Robert Wagner, who wrote the National Labor Relations Act and the Social Security Act, acknowledged the importance of the railroad legislation in fostering his desire to create a national retirement system, which he believed would foster economic stability by increasing the purchasing power of a growing segment of the population: the elderly. Establishing a pension system for railroad workers provided a much-needed " . . . laboratory for experiment . . ." that would " . . . blaze the way for full treatment of the problem."[29]

In Chapter 9 I examine the labor banking movement. The Brotherhood of Locomotive Engineers attempted to establish labor banks to move labor's battles from the " . . . picket line to the board room." Other unions followed the lead of the BLE, whose president, Warren Stone, became a symbol of the labor banking movement. Ultimately, the BLE's financial empire crashed and an ill-timed investment in Florida real estate nearly destroyed the union. The union's foray into banking demonstrates not only its activism, but is also labor's boldest attempt to move beyond its traditional boundaries while remaining within a capitalist framework. Railroad labor did not view itself as part of an American working class, but rather as part of the burgeoning middle class.

Railroading Prior to World War I

By the time that World War I began, working for railroads had lost much of its frontier quality and romance. Railroading retained some of its luster, but the hard edge was gone. Increased government regulations, improved personnel practices, and a greater drive for efficiency and safety were largely responsible for these changes. Operating trains was still a hazardous occupation, but improved technology had made it safer. Americans were beginning a new love affair with automobiles, although most toddlers in the twenty-first century can still identify a train and know that it makes a "choo-choo" sound, which is a testament to the continued importance of trains and the industry's significance in American history and folklore. Automobiles were about to replace railroads in the hearts of Americans and as the driving force of the nation's industry.

The workaday world of railroaders had changed immensely over the previous century. Employment requirements, which were loosely defined and haphazardly enforced during the first half-century of railroading, had become more stringent. In the nineteenth century, when industry officials considered the question of employee qualifications they often spoke in vague moralistic terms: employees should be "sober," "prompt," "honest," and "exhibit gentlemanly behavior towards passengers."[1] When hiring, one exacting standard that carriers upheld in all but extreme situations was that workers could not have been dismissed for violation of Rule G, which forbade alcohol consumption on the job.

Of course employers still desired these qualities in the twentieth century, and hiring procedures had evolved over the preceding decades that allowed carriers to more often achieve their objective. In the middle of the nineteenth century, carriers decentralized their hiring procedure, delegating hiring to local officials to remind operatives from whence authority emanated.[2] By the beginning of the twentieth century, increasingly stringent hiring regulations were more uniform. Job candidates often had to fill out a multipage application and undergo a physical examination. As on current employment applications, employers often sought information regarding the applicants' education and work experience, and some applications contained a section that dealt with prior injuries. In the nineteenth century, however, family and personal connections were often the most important factors in gaining employment.

Fluidity of employment opportunities was another characteristic of nineteenth-century railroading. In the first decades of the industry, operatives moved deftly among various jobs. Early accounts of railroad work are filled with reminiscences of working at various jobs depending upon the road's need. Men often had experience switching, braking, firing, and conducting. Nineteenth-century railroaders who frequently switched jobs were known as "boomers," but by the twentieth century these vagabonds were less in evidence.[3]

The early career of A. F. Whitney, future Brotherhood of Railroad Trainmen president, is illustrative of late-nineteenth-century boomers. In August 1890, Whitney, then seventeen, said he was twenty-one, and the Illinois Central's trainmaster in Cherokee, Iowa, hired him as a brakeman. A brakeman or trainman at the turn of the century was of course responsible for braking the cars of the train, which meant climbing on top of each car and setting the brakes by hand. Additionally, a brakeman would couple and uncouple cars, set necessary warning flags, and inspect the train for any mechanical problems.

Whitney was laid off the following March and rehired in July 1891. He worked for sixteen days before quitting when he got mad at his train's conductor for yelling at him. On August 22, 1891, he found employment on the Fremont, Elkhorn, and Missouri Valley Railroad and was laid off less than a month later. After a stint husking corn, the Illinois Central again hired him as a brakeman. This time his employment lasted from December 24, 1891, to February 20, 1892, when the trainmaster fired him because he forgot to remove the green flags from the back of his caboose when he went to lunch. He was not employed on railroads again until November 1892, when the Chicago and Northwestern Railroad hired him. The following March

Whitney lost two fingers on his left hand while trying to couple cars using the link-and-pin coupler. The company paid him $45 for his lost fingers. Because of the economic depression, Whitney worked as a painter and wallpaper hanger for several years before reentering the train service in 1895. He worked steadily for more than five years before going to work for the BRT in 1901.[4]

Being Promoted

By the twentieth century job classifications had become more rigid, and unions gained greater control of the promotion process, making it difficult for carriers to hire an engineer or a conductor from outside the company. It was customary throughout most of the industry's history for a man to work as a fireman before being promoted to engineer, and as a brakeman before becoming a conductor. As positions became more difficult to secure because of decreasing fluidity, the qualifications to gain employment, and later promotions, became more stringent. Boomers were less common, at least on the large carriers that had union contracts with the operating brotherhoods.

Firing was physically one of the most demanding jobs in the industry. Steam locomotives had a Paul Bunyan–like appetite for water and coal; firemen were largely responsible for fulfilling their hunger. They were responsible for shoveling as much as ten or twenty tons of coal into the boiler during a trip. Some locomotives had a mechanical stoker. It was the fireman's responsibility to monitor the stoker to maintain the proper kind of fire—he might have to increase or decrease its speed depending upon the operating needs. If it broke down he had to be prepared to begin shoveling coal himself. On a steam locomotive he was also responsible for wetting down the coal, breaking up large chunks of coal and pulling it forward from the back of the tender, shaking the grates, and taking on coal and water. Some railroads used trackside water towers, but a few used track pans, and the fireman was responsible for lowering the scoop, which could take on thousands of gallons, as the train passed over the pan. Firemen monitored steam gauges and watched for signals on the left side of the train, which on locomotives by the 1920s was almost invisible to engineers. Watching for signals and highway crossings was especially difficult in inclement weather.[5]

To graduate to the "right side of the cab" and become an engineer, a fireman had to pass a series of exams over a period of years. If he failed, he would not be retained so long as qualified men were available. The Brotherhood of Locomotive Firemen and Engineers booklet *Feeding the Iron Hog* notes that the requirements of carriers varied, but outlined the criteria of one railroad. After six months, a fireman took an exam consisting of more than two hundred questions dealing with nearly all facets of the industry. Six months later he took a second exam dealing with firing and fuel economy, with additional questions concerning air brakes. At the end of the second year, he took another test that dealt with firing and air brakes. The final exam included nearly one thousand questions. Additionally, firemen and engineers had to acquaint themselves with a variety of locomotives—forty-four under the Whyte system of classification.[6]

In contrast to the stringent requirements of the twentieth century, J. Harvey Reed, while working on the Wabash in 1871, moved across the cab by answering one question, and in a flippant manner at that. The master mechanic asked him what tools he deemed necessary to have with him on a run. Reed responded, "A whole shop if I were on the wrecks on the St. Louis Division."[7]

By the twentieth century men who became engineers had spent many years on trains honing their skills. It was not uncommon for firemen, even after they passed all the exams, to continue to fire for more than a decade. They continued as firemen in part because advancing technology allowed one bigger, stronger locomotive to replace several older machines. Between 1919 and 1926 the average tractive power of locomotives increased from thirty-six thousand pounds to forty thousand pounds.[8] Each locomotive and each train it pulled had unique operating characteristics based on weight and length. Engineers also had to know how each train handled in different types of terrain.

According to lore, in the early days of railroading a conductor and an engineer fought over who controlled the train; the conductor won. Thus, conductors were responsible for operation of the train. To become a conductor one generally had to work first as a brakeman. By the twentieth century, the brakeman had to pass an exam before being promoted to conductor. If he failed, he could retake the test in ninety days. If a candidate failed a second time, the carrier usually terminated him.[9] In freight service the conductor was responsible for delivering and picking up freight and for adding required cars during the run. Yard conductors were responsible for assembling trains prior to their dispatch.

The conductors' call of "all aboard!" and then passing up and down the aisle punching passengers' tickets are iconic. Beyond those two duties conductors on passenger service were responsible for the train's overall operation. They executed operational instructions, helped passengers, and made sure that operating rules were observed. Conductors and engineers typically started on freight service and were then promoted to passenger trains.

Gradually, a seniority system emerged that governed promotions and decreased fluidity. Seniority systems first appeared prior to the Civil War, and in 1875 the first written contract of the Brotherhood of Locomotive Engineers (BLE) incorporated seniority practices. At first, the regulations were simple. By the second decade of the twentieth century, they had become quite elaborate, covering every conceivable question that could arise: promotion, demotion, date of seniority, merging of railroads, transfers, leaving the job, new lines or extensions, posting seniority lists, review of seniority complaints, reemployment, promotion to official positions, electric service, and other matters connected with the protection of the engineer's employment tenure.[10] Procedures varied, but for many railroaders—not just engineers and conductors—the seniority system dictated the course of their careers.

Operatives initially welcomed the seniority system, but by the 1920s it was both a blessing and a curse. Problems arose because of the restrictive nature of hiring in the industry. When a young man began working as a brakeman or a fireman, the number of runs he received depended upon his seniority. Work was often irregular until he gained some seniority. If he remained employed for the same carrier, he could look forward to attaining a steady run, and the benefits of continual work and regular pay. The difficulty arose when he gained enough seniority to become a conductor or an engineer, or when he could be promoted from freight service to passenger runs. The operative went from having the most seniority to having the least. Consequently, a promotion often meant irregular runs and decreased pay, so it was not uncommon for a man to turn it down.[11]

In the early days of railroading, a man could expect to be promoted within several years, or he could simply quit and move on to find a better job. As the nineteenth century drew to a close, operatives found the paths to promotion difficult to traverse. In the early decades of the twentieth century, a fireman might have to work ten or more years before being promoted; it was not unheard of for a man to fire more than twenty years without a promotion.[12]

Increased Safety

Railroading was dangerous for both operatives and passengers in the nineteenth century. Compiling injury statistics for the century is extremely problematic. Figures gathered by state commissions and individual carriers provide insight but are clearly limited. In Connecticut and Massachusetts between the late 1850s and 1880 trainmen accounted for 60 and 55 percent of injuries, respectively, and 57 and 64 percent of fatalities.[13] For the decade of 1874 to 1884, men in the train service on the Illinois Central had a 1 in 20 chance of being injured and 1 in 120 was killed. Men in the switching service were more likely to be hurt or killed. One in 7 was injured and 1 in 90 was killed.[14] Passengers were also at risk. In the 1880s Massachusetts averaged 208 deaths annually, and the accident rate was worse in other states. Passenger safety increased threefold between the early 1890s and the years just before World War I, by which time there was less than one fatality for each one hundred million passenger-miles of service.[15] Advanced technology such as air brakes, automatic couplers, and improved communications could not remove all hazards, but safety standards had generally improved by the twentieth century.

Braking was one of the most dangerous jobs. Ideally each brakeman would operate the brakes of two or three cars, but they were often responsible for twice that number.[16] When the engineer blew the whistle calling for brakes down, brakemen were to scramble up ladders and over roofs to their assigned cars to set the brakes. The brakeman on top of a car was in an extremely vulnerable position. In winter, ice and snow posed severe hazards. He also faced rain, high winds, and darkness. Brakemen had to remain vigilant to avoid the most dangerous hazards: overhead obstructions that often knocked them from cars, breaking their limbs and worse.

Another dangerous job was coupling cars. While the task could be deadly, the men who performed it were more likely to suffer severed fingers when they handled coupling devices that did not line up perfectly. Using the older link-and-pin system, switchmen often had to jimmy one side or the other so that it lined up properly with the other side. Most operatives preferred to use their hands instead of the paddle device that had been developed. One way that personnel officials would determine if a job applicant had experience was to ask to see his hands; a missing finger or two was proof of his experience. A nineteenth-century brakeman noted that using the link-and-pin

Figure 1. While safer than in the past, by the early twentieth century railroading was still a dangerous occupation. This collision occurred in November 1906. By permission of the Kheel Center for Labor Management Documentation and Archives, United Transportation Union Collection, Cornell University.

system required skill and perfect coordination of mind and muscle, because " . . . a man only lived long enough to make one mistake."[17] Congress passed the Safety Appliance Act in 1893 requiring carriers to install automatic brakes and coupling devices. These devices had been available for more than two decades, but many carriers refused to install them.[18]

Men in the cab were a little safer. Early enginemen did not have the benefit of cover because the traveling public opposed it, but within a decade cabs appeared on engines. Operatives faced sparks and the hazards of boilers that could explode. All trainmen and passengers faced frequent derailments, collisions, and the occasional bridge collapse. Equipment sometimes failed, but human error was often the cause of accidents. Because trains did not have onboard communications, they moved according to telegraphic messages and strict instructions, which could be lost or misinterpreted. They could also change after a train was under way. Head-on collisions or rear-end wrecks were not uncommon.[19] The career of Harry French is illustrative. He was in five train wrecks in a five-week period, and although he faced suspensions for each, he was not hurt. The causes of the wrecks help to illuminate some of the problems railroaders faced. Two of the accidents occurred because of equipment failure: a broken axle and a broken rail. A train running past a signalman and a man's failure to properly set a siding switch accounted for two more crashes. The fifth accident resulted from a stack of hay being blown onto the tracks.[20] French also survived a bridge collapse. As old, wooden bridges were replaced by steel structures in the late nineteenth century, safety improved.

Railroaders faced these dangers daily and sometimes could not even look forward to regular paydays. Because of cash deficiencies carriers sometimes paid in company script or had workers submit their bills directly to the railroad for payment. Reed writes, "The road's financial status was as full of promises as a rainbow . . . one got accustomed to living on rarified promises."[21]

As in all industries in the nineteenth century, long hours marked the work life of men in the train service. Train schedules were poorly structured, and neither officials nor employees felt a strong compulsion to run the trains on time. Dispatching methods were crude; trains often sat idle waiting for running orders. Engines that broke down also caused delays, or, because coal and water supplies were not properly spaced, engines were forced to run ahead to resupply, temporarily abandoning the train. Because steep grades were common, trains often had to be broken into two or more sections and brought separately over the grade. Long hours and tired crews contributed to countless accidents.[22] While delays affected all operating employees, they weighed most heavily on the conductor since he was in charge and would have to deal with frustrated, angry passengers.

Emergence of Unions

Generally, nineteenth-century industrialists crushed unions. Carriers grudgingly accepted organization for engineers, firemen, conductors, and trainmen because the four brotherhoods that represented these operatives— founded between 1863 and 1883—were initially fraternal organizations, not traditional labor unions.[23] Their primary function was to provide insurance that private companies were reluctant to issue. Further, each organization held a generally dim view of strikes. Engineers often entered the train service as firemen, and conductors as brakemen, but they often maintained their membership in the first union they joined. Thus some engineers were mem-

Figure 2. Founded in September 1883, the BRT was one of the "operating brotherhoods" and independent of the AFL. In 1969, it merged with the BLFE, SUNA, and ORC to form the United Transportation Union. Today the UTU represents 125,000 members. By permission of the Kheel Center for Labor Management Documentation and Archives, BRT Collection, Cornell University.

bers of the Brotherhood of Locomotive Firemen and Enginemen (BLFE). Likewise some conductors remained in the Brotherhood of Railroad Trainmen (BRT). Early in the twentieth century, all four unions had organized the majority of operatives in their respective fields. The Brotherhood of Locomotive Engineers (BLE) and the Order of Railway Conductors (ORC) each had approximately 90 percent of the men under contract, while the BLFE and the BRT had organized 75 and 65 percent, respectively.[24]

While these statistics indicate a high level of organization, it should be noted that the unions were highly restrictive, limiting their membership to white males. The four operating brotherhoods constitutionally barred blacks from joining. Many African-Americans and other minority workers were crucial to the operation of American railroads, and most often worked in the hardest, most dangerous tasks in the industry. Although black workers often found employment as firemen or brakemen, it was on unorganized, small roads because the major carriers had contracts with the four operating unions. Of course, African-American workers were not paid as well as their white peers. Restrictions against African-Americans—except in extreme circumstances like the world wars—remained in place until the 1950s and 1960s, when federal and state judges declared such restrictions unconstitutional.[25]

The growth of railroads further stimulated the transportation and price revolutions that had been under way since early in the nineteenth century. The nation's economy was becoming truly national in character. The growing dependence on railroads prompted a great deal of concern, especially among farmers. Many Americans were especially concerned because, in their view, railroad competition was declining, and the carriers were coming increasingly under the domination of eastern bankers.[26] People's historic fear of monopolies was clearly evident.[27] A useful barometer of the growing importance of railroads is that between 1868 and 1886 congressmen introduced more than 150 regulatory bills. Perhaps more significantly, the large number of bills indicates the gradual decline of laissez-faire economic policies. That Congress was even willing to consider regulatory measures was an important step in the evolution of the modern state's economic policy.

Early railroads, however, were largely the creatures of state charters or local boosterism, and so it was the states that first addressed regulatory issues. Rhode Island, in 1839, created the nation's first railroad commission. Connecticut, Maine, and New York also created regulatory commissions before the Civil War. Regulation remained minimal prior to the war. The antebellum experience demonstrated that legislators and judges were not qualified to supervise or regulate the industry.

Massachusetts ushered in a new era in 1869, when it created a more powerful regulatory body chaired by Charles Francis Adams Jr. The Bay State's commission had the power to investigate accidents and to determine if railroads were complying with their charter obligations. Carriers were required to turn over information requested by the commission, and commissioners could recommend—but not order—changes or repairs in either operations or rates to companies. Enforcement depended upon persuasion and public opinion.[28]

In 1887, President Grover Cleveland signed the Interstate Commerce Act in response to strikes the previous year. The legislation created the Interstate Commerce Commission (ICC), which had the power to regulate railroad rates and competition. Passage of the Interstate Commerce Act indicated that Congress recognized the public character of railroads and demonstrated its determination that the carriers operate with the public interest in mind.[29] The new legislation was hardly the cure that proponents sought, however, in part because rates and competition were not the only problems that the railroad industry faced.

Maintaining peaceful labor relations was another important component in the railroad equation. Strikes in the nineteenth century were noted for their violence. In the Railway Strike of 1877, twenty-six people were killed in Pittsburgh, and strikers destroyed approximately $5 million of railroad property. Nationally, railroads suffered around $10 million in losses. Although the national government did not pass labor legislation immediately after the violence of 1877, it was the most violent outbreak of labor unrest in the railroad industry to date, which was fraught with worker discontent.[30]

During the Gilded Age the economy grew to become truly national. For the first time, a strike in a particular industry—especially railroads—could have nationwide ramifications. Americans depended on railroads to transport everything from soup to nuts, but the U.S. Mail was in some respects the most precious cargo, and not simply because railroads offered the most efficient mode of transportation. Because many railroads transported mail, the federal government was able to step in during labor disputes, ostensibly to insure that mail service continued without interruption.

Because tranquil labor relations were essential to the national economy, Congress enacted three laws between 1888 and 1913 to foster resolution of railroad labor disputes.[31] Congress looked upon itself as guardian of the public interest; consequently its approach was to provide machinery to facilitate, but not force, a solution to conflicts that the parties could not settle in private negotiations.[32] Congress passed the Act of 1888, which provided two means of adjudicating disputes that threatened to interrupt interstate commerce: voluntary arbitration and investigation.[33] The Act, which was similar to a proposal suggested by President Cleveland in 1886, provided that if the parties could not solve their differences, they should agree to arbitration. Management and labor were each to name one arbitrator. Those arbitrators would name the third member of the panel who was to serve as the chairman. Neither party, however, was bound by the arbitration board's ruling. Public opinion and cooperation were to be the foundation of dispute resolution. The president gained the power to appoint a commission if either party or a state official requested it. The commission was also to help settle a dispute if it threatened interstate commerce.[34] During the decade the Act was in force, its arbitration provisions were never used, and only during the Pullman strike did the president appoint a special commission.[35]

In 1898, Congress enacted a new labor law, the Erdman Act. It empowered the federal government to engage in mediation, conciliation, and arbitration in those railroad labor disputes that, significantly, only involved the operating employees. If an unsettled dispute threatened to disrupt interstate commerce, the United States Commissioner of Labor and the chairman of the ICC were to choose a third person, and the three were to act to bring about arbitration. Any arbitration award was compulsory, but only for one year. The law also prohibited yellow-dog contracts and other types of discrimination against union members. The Erdman Act was used infrequently, and the parties were generally not satisfied with its provisions.[36]

Congress enacted the Newlands Act in 1913 to replace the Erdman Act because of a threatened strike. The new legislation was built on the principle of arbitration. The Newlands Act created a Board of Mediation and Conciliation, consisting of a full-time commissioner appointed by the president and two part-time commissioners appointed from other government agencies. The board's decisions were not legally enforceable. Still, between 1913 and 1919 the board handled 148 cases involving 620,000 employees. Seventy cases were settled by mediation alone, twenty-one by mediation and arbitration, and nineteen by mutual agreement of the parties involved.[37] The great increase in traffic created by World War I, and especially after America's entry in April 1917, overwhelmed the machinery of the Newlands Act.

Conclusion

Railroad labor legislation passed between 1888 and 1913 met with limited success, and the railroad unions had no voice in its creation. The federal government provided the machinery to facilitate dispute resolution but did not require parties to participate.[38] The unions generally remained outside the political arena as they had historically, but that was about to change. In the period between World War I and the New Deal, organized railroad labor was to play a far more active role in shaping legislation. The pre–World War I attempts to regulate railroad labor, however, were important, because together they established the government's central role in maintaining labor peace—at least for a small segment of the workforce. Carriers also had to accept government intervention, thus relinquishing a small amount of managerial prerogative to the federal government. Pre-war attempts to govern railroad labor relations created models for subsequent legislation, but they did nothing to politicize railroad workers.

The Great War and its Aftermath

World War I was a watershed for the railroad unions. It brought them together in an informal alliance, led by the BLE, BLFE, BRT, and the ORC. The other unions, most of which belonged to the RED, generally followed the lead of the brotherhoods. Their members were among the most skilled, best paid workers in America and thus positioned to lead American labor.

The federal government took control of the nation's railroads in December 1917 in an effort to keep troops moving and supplies flowing. The enabling legislation required that the carriers be returned to private control within twenty-one months of the end of hostilities. At the war's conclusion, the "railroad question" was one of the most pressing before Congress, which seized on the opportunity to rather dramatically expand the regulatory role of the federal government.

Railroads Before Federal Control, 1914–1917

During the war, the American railroad network reached its zenith. In 1916 railroad mileage peaked at 254,037, and the railroads employed approximately 1.7 million men and women—or about 4 percent of employed Americans.[1] The carriers struggled to meet wartime demands. In 1915 there were three hundred thousand more freight car loadings than the previous year. In 1916 the ton-miles over which railroads transported goods increased 32 percent. Labor struggled to meet the increased demands.

The operating brotherhoods used the exigent circumstances to make significant gains. In the summer of 1916, they demanded the eight-hour day and that their pay remain based on a ten-hour day. First the U.S. Board of Mediation and then President Woodrow Wilson failed to negotiate a settlement. Finally, Wilson asked Congress to legislate a solution. It responded quickly with the Adamson Act, which went into effect on January 1, 1917, and granted the unions' demands for the eight-hour day. The carriers refused to comply until the courts ruled on it. A strike was narrowly averted in March, when the carriers yielded on the same afternoon that the U.S. Supreme Court, in a 5–4 ruling, upheld the law.[2] Into the 1920s railroad officials and the public criticized the Adamson Act and urged that it be repealed.[3]

The railroad crisis grew more serious when the United States entered the war in April 1917. The carriers tried to meet it through voluntary measures. Daniel Willard, president of the Baltimore and Ohio Railroad, and chairman and transportation expert on the Advisory Commission of the Council of National Defense, convened a meeting of nearly seven hundred railroad presidents on April 11, 1917. The presidents signed a resolution agreeing to contribute to the war effort by running their lines as though they constituted " . . . a continental railway system."[4] The executives named a five-man board headed by Fairfax Harrison, president of the Southern Railway, to coordinate their activities. The executives' voluntary efforts were ineffective. Perhaps most significantly, they never completely lost sight of their own company's interests.[5]

The crisis was much worse by autumn. Because the predominant flow of material was to eastern ports, and there were few goods to ship back to the hinterland, a car shortage grew increasingly acute; by November 1 it was 158,000. Low morale and high turnover among workers compounded railroads' logistical headaches.[6] Operatives left to work in higher-paying war industries or to join the military. When the federal government took control of the carriers, some companies reported a 12.5 percent shortage in their shop force.[7] As the year drew to a close, severe weather exacerbated these problems.

The carriers were not entirely to blame for their inability to meet the transportation crisis.[8] By the first decade of the twentieth century, the ICC had brought an end to the internecine railroad competition of the previous century, which American industrial leaders welcomed.[9] But in the fluid circumstances of the war, ICC regulation was of less value. Wages continued to rise, but the carriers got little relief from the ICC, which controlled rates, making it difficult for the roads to pay competitive wages or to purchase necessary equipment. As European demand for American food and material increased, ton-mileage for freight traffic rose 43 percent during 1914 and 1915. Efficient operation was increasingly difficult. In 1917, the carriers appealed to the ICC for a freight-rate hike of 15 percent, but were granted only a token increase. Operating expenses were rising so rapidly that even if the ICC had granted the request, it would not have been enough.[10] On December 5, 1917, the ICC submitted a special report to Congress recommending federal operation of the railroads.[11]

President Wilson acted quickly using power granted to him by the Federal Possession and Control Act; he placed the roads under federal control on December 28. Specific details were articulated in the Railroad Control Act, which Congress passed in March 1918. It stipulated that the annual compensation to the lines should be no more than the average net operating income for the three years ending June 30, 1917. The government was responsible for maintenance and repairs, and property was to be returned " . . . in substantially good repair and in substantially as complete equipment as it was at the beginning of federal control." The expenses of federal control and operation were to be met with a revolving fund of $500 million created for that purpose. Finally, the law required that the carriers be returned to their owners within twenty-one months following ratification of a peace treaty.[12] Unions generally supported federal operation and benefitted from it. Labor's wartime advances were at the crux of the conflict between labor and management for most of the ensuing decade.

Railroad Labor Under Federal Control, 1917–1920

Reformers hoped the United States Railroad Administration (USRA) would implement their ideas of economy, efficiency, and service. President Wilson appointed William McAdoo Director General of the USRA; he staffed the USRA with men long conditioned by their experience running railroads as private enterprises. Initially, labor leaders were excluded, but one exception was the appointment of W. S. Carter, president of the BLFE, as head of the Division of Labor.[13] A second union executive who would be at the center of labor's political activities after the war, William H. Johnston of the International Association of Machinists, served on the National Labor Relations Board. The presence of Carter and Johnston in the federal wartime bureaucracy gave operatives reason to be somewhat optimistic.

By the time the USRA assumed control of the railroads, the labor situa-

Figure 3. A. B. Garrettson, ORC president. By permission of the Kheel Center for Labor Management Documentation and Archives, ORC and Brakemen, Collection, Cornell University.

tion had become serious. Inflation had been steadily eroding wages, and in the autumn of 1917 the union representatives, led by A. B. Garrettson, president of the ORC, and W. G. Lee, president of the BRT, met with carriers' representatives to discuss the problem. Simultaneously, the Switchmens Union of North America (SUNA) was meeting in Chicago and passed a resolution that called for a 50 percent wage increase. On November 1 the *New York Times* reported that the three unions were prepared to strike if their wage demands were not met. The carriers proposed arbitration, but the unions demanded mediation.[14]

The USRA quickly addressed the wage question. McAdoo appointed a commission, chaired by Franklin K. Lane, secretary of the interior, to investigate. The Lane Commission concluded that the cost of living had increased 40 percent between December 1915 and December 1917, and that substantial wage increases were due railroad workers, with those paid the least receiving the greatest increases.[15]

Labor relations changed because the USRA circumvented progressive-era dispute-resolution agencies, creating three National Boards of Adjustment. The boards, which had equal representation from labor and management, were to decide all questions of discipline and application of USRA orders when local parties could not reach an agreement.[16] Union representatives were to bring unsettled disputes to the USRA Division of Labor, which would ask the appropriate Board of Adjustment to hear the case. Technically, the boards were to hear only cases on roads where pre-war union agreements existed, but in reality they heard cases from all carriers under federal control. Labor unions benefited because through the boards they gained greater uniformity of work rules, which the carriers vigorously opposed.

Labor gained another long-sought victory when the USRA issued General Order No. 8 on February 21, 1918, which forbade railroads from discriminating against operatives who joined labor organizations. The four operating brotherhoods had contracts with most carriers, but they accounted for only 19 percent of the railroad labor force, or about 330,000 workers. Union membership among the remainder of the industry was relatively low. Unorganized workers quickly joined unions, but locals did not make agreements with the carriers; terms were set by government fiat. Labor leaders worried about maintaining their positions when federal control ended. This was, of course, the scenario that left some labor leaders, including Sam Gompers of the AFL, unenthusiastic about government regulation.

Railroad workers benefited from federal control. Specifically, they gained wage increases, union recognition, standardized work rules—including seniority and minute classification of job descriptions in the shops—elimination of piece work, and equality of pay for both women and African-Americans in some jobs.[17] Women and African-Americans were still far from being treated equally in all aspects of the industry. The number of women working on the nation's railroads reached one hundred thousand in October 1918—about two and a half times more than pre-war levels. Unions, however, still largely barred African-Americans and women.[18] Gains made by women and African-American workers were short lived.

These changes were important for all railroad operatives, not just the four independent brotherhoods. They marked the high-water mark of union strength and power in the pre–New Deal era. When the war ended the unions were keenly aware that industrialists would use all their resources to regain lost power. Gompers, addressing the Pan American Labor Conference in Laredo, TX, just days after the war ended, said that labor would resist the attempt by employers to take away wartime gains " . . . to the uttermost."[19] The desire of the unions to maintain their improved position in the face of strong employer opposition in the post-war years was the basis for their electoral and lobbying efforts in the years between World War I and the New Deal. Although the federal government had taken an active role in railroad labor relations prior to the war, it was through the agency of the unions in the interwar years that its role increased.

In the aftermath of the war, railroad workers were eager to continue government control. In December 1918, the RED executive committee adopted a resolution that officers prepare a letter and ballot " . . . for the purpose of securing an expression of the members on the question of Government Ownership" versus private control. The RED reported that 308,186 members voted. Six unions' figures were recorded. A stunning 99.5 percent favored government control. Only 1,466 union members voted against it.[20]

Post-War Debate

With the end of hostilities came the question of what to do with America's federalized railroad system. Senator Albert B. Cummins (R-IA) thought that, with the possible exception of the League of Nations controversy, the re-adjustment of railroad relations was the most difficult question facing the United States.[21] His colleague, Atlee Pomerene (D-OH), agreed.[22] As chairman of the Interstate and Foreign Commerce Committee, Cummins was a central figure in the coming debate.

Most everyone agreed that the pre-war system had failed. It was clear that workers would not readily relinquish their wartime gains. Previously, railroad labor exerted little influence over public policy. However, during the war, in certain situations, organized labor forced action. Union leaders had tasted a bit of success and were determined to maintain it. The carriers were equally resolute; they wanted to turn the clock back to the status quo ante bellum.

In his annual message to Congress, published in the *New York Times* December 3, 1918, just one day before he sailed to Europe for the Versailles Peace Conference, President Wilson wrote, "The question which causes me the greatest concern is the question of the policy to be adopted toward the railroads." He made it clear that he had no specific plan or even clear objective. He ended his statement by writing, "The one conclusion that I am ready to state with confidence is that it would be a disservice alike to the country and to the owners of the railroads to return to the old conditions unmodified."[23]

The debate over the "railroad question" began in earnest in January 1919 when the Senate Interstate and Foreign Commerce Committee began its hearings, which continued with a few interruptions until October. The House Committee hearings began in July.[24] While Wilson had no specific plan, McAdoo thought the situation was ripe for experimentation. In December 1918, he wrote letters to Cummins, who chaired the Senate Interstate and Foreign Commerce Committee, and to his counterpart in the House, John Esch (R-WI) expressing his belief that federal control should be extended for five years. He argued that extended control would help the roads over the inevitable difficulties of post-war reconstruction and allow the USRA to proceed with necessary improvements. Before the war, in the fall of 1915, one-sixth of the nation's railroad miles—or more than forty-thousand miles, with capitalization of $2.25 billion—were in receivership. Clearly, labor issues were not the only concern. McAdoo feared that Republicans would use administration of the railroads, which most of the carriers' partisans thought a dismal failure, as a campaign issue in 1920. Walker D. Hines succeeded McAdoo, who resigned from the Cabinet and USRA early in 1919, and he recommended one of two courses of action: for the administration to maintain control for three to five years or to return the roads to private control promptly.[25]

Neither McAdoo nor Hines had much influence in the Republican-controlled Congress. Government control beyond the statutory limit of twenty-one months after the ratification of the peace treaty was anathema to many congressmen and, of course, to railroad executives. In all, there were seven major plans submitted to Congress.[26] The pre-war assertion that railroad regulation should encourage efficient operation in an integrated transportation system, converged with the war experience of federal operation and popular notions of scientific management. Most of the plans assumed that the new regulation would transcend mere adjudication of labor disputes by encouraging both efficiency and harmony.[27] Clearly, the progressive impulse was not completely dead.

When the hearings began, labor executives were not sure which plan to support. There was strong sentiment that federal control should continue. Grand Chief Warren Stone of the BLE asked union counsel Glenn Plumb to attend the hearings. While there, Plumb wrote his own proposal, the Plumb Plan, which the unions eventually endorsed. Plumb believed that the railroads were a public utility cursed by a " . . . low degree of managerial skill" because they had always been exploited by Wall Street financiers.[28]

The Plumb Plan called for the federal government to acquire full control of the railroads by paying stock and bond owners the court-determined value of their investment. Plumb estimated that the railroads' improved efficiency would result in annual savings of more than three-quarters of a billion dollars. It also proposed the creation of a nonprofit corporation by the federal government, with no capital stock and no bonds, which was to equally represent the public interest, railroad management, and labor on its board of directors. Rates were to be established at a level intended to cover expenses. If, through improved efficiency, the corporation turned a profit, half of the dividends were to be distributed to employees, and half would belong to the public. The plan called for labor disputes to be settled by a ten-member board; operating officials and employees would each name five men. Unsolved disputes were to be settled by the Board of Directors.[29]

Plumb presented his plan to union leaders shortly after the hearings began. The executives were impressed, prompting one to write that it was the " . . . most feasible, practical and advantageous plan that could be devised." They unanimously approved it, hired Plumb to promote it at a monthly salary of $1,000, and created the Plumb Plan League and a monthly publication, *Railroad Democracy*. To promote the proposal, the unions were taxed based on the number of members, which gave the League an initial budget of about $61,000.[30] With the exception of the BRT, which withdrew from the League rather than pay its tax of about $7,000, railroad labor remained firmly behind the Plumb Plan. Formation of the Plumb Plan League and *Railroad Democracy* were important cooperative steps for the railroad labor organizations in their quest to influence labor policies through the ballot box.

The executives soon asked former Democratic Colorado congressman Edward Keating to edit *Railroad Democracy*. He was first elected in 1912, but like many Democrats he lost his bid for reelection in 1918. He quickly convinced labor leaders to scrap the monthly *Railroad Democracy* for a weekly newspaper, *Labor*. He insisted that *Labor* concentrate on union news, labor parties abroad, and work conditions. The publication constantly offered a progressive critique of American society. Keating wanted the paper, which he edited until his retirement in 1953, to appeal to all friends of labor.[31]

Keating was an excellent choice as editor. Before entering Congress he worked on newspapers for more than two decades, beginning as a teenager in 1889 in Denver; eventually he purchased the *Pueblo Leader*. His first political involvement was working as a ward boss for the Populist party in the

1890s before he was old enough to vote. He became a Democrat when, behind William Jennings Bryan, the party abandoned the gold standard.[32] During his tenure in Congress, he cosponsored the Keating-Owen Child Labor Bill.

The union leaders showed little political savvy in their support of the Plumb Plan. In the aftermath of World War I, the United States experienced a spasm of violence aimed at political radicals, unionists, and anyone else deemed un-American. During the Red Scare, strikes were crushed, violence was common, and immigrant radicals, like Emma Goldman, were deported. Even in a less charged political environment, the Plumb Plan would have had little chance of being enacted. Outside of organized labor, a few farm organizations, and a small band of intellectuals the Plumb Plan received little attention. To most Americans any solution that involved further government ownership smacked of Bolshevism. Many thought the plan was socialist-inspired, a charge that Keating flatly denied: "Of course it wasn't socialism. Of all the railroad leaders of that period that I knew, but one was a Socialist. The others were just plain Americans. I believe most were Republicans."[33] Once it became obvious that the Plumb Plan had no chance of passing, labor leaders pushed for extended federal control as McAdoo and Hines had advocated.

The political reality was that no plans except those proposed by the chairs of the respective Interstate and Foreign Commerce Committees, Esch and Cummins, would receive much support. Cummins' bill, which had more widespread support within the GOP than Esch's, shows how his thinking had been shaped by scientific management theories of the day. Greater efficiency was the key. The best way to achieve it was for railroads to consolidate, a compromise between public and private ownership. Consolidation into twenty to thirty-five national systems would be voluntary if achieved within seven years and mandatory after that time. He believed that consolidation would eliminate the constant rate controversies and allow managers to apply scientific management principles. Profits in excess of 6 percent were to be split between the carrier and the government and put into a trust fund to be used to finance improvements. The regulation of securities was placed under federal control. The ICC was to remain, but its powers would be restricted. A five-member Transportation Board appointed by the president was to administer government-held funds for capital improvement, rule upon proposals to construct new lines, and perform other administrative tasks.[34] Cummins' proposal was surprisingly progressive with its call for government-regulated competition, which included limited profits.

The unions may have found the Cummins bill acceptable except for the labor clause, which called for committees of four employees and four management representatives to settle disputes. The new boards would not be national, which labor opposed. If the committee could not resolve the conflict, it was to be referred to the Transportation Board. The bill also outlawed strikes and lockouts. Cummins said that labor would give up the right to strike in exchange for " . . . an enlightened government."[35] Grand Chief Stone of the BLE called it the most vicious piece of legislation in recent years.[36] Clearly, organized labor would lose much of its wartime power.

Esch's version, crafted largely by ICC partisans, " . . . amounted to a classic exercise in time-warp politics. It sought to restore the *status quo ante-bellum* with the roads run privately under strict ICC regulation."[37] Consolidation, which would not be mandatory, would take place only with the commission's approval. The ICC would control stocks, bonds, and expenditure of their proceeds. Labor defeated a no-strike clause in the first draft, but there were other aspects of the proposal it found odious, one of which was that adjustment boards would not settle disputes between carriers and nonoperating brotherhoods, which would have eliminated an essential component of wartime organization. The proposal also abandoned voluntarism, which had marked earlier railroad labor legislation, and gave the judiciary authority to enforce rulings.[38]

The conference committee began its hearings at the end of December 1919, and soon reached an agreement. The Esch-Cummins Bill, officially the Transportation Act of 1920, went into effect on March 1. It was unique in that it squarely inserted the federal government into the middle of the industry by abandoning the voluntary characteristics of previous laws and providing for adjustment boards to handle disputes. It immediately created controversy. The ICC was to establish a "fair" rate of return determined to be 5.5 percent. It encouraged—but did not require—mergers that were deemed in the public interest, and established a fund drawn from the profits in excess of 6 percent from sound carriers to aid financially ailing railways. The new law also gave the ICC the power to regulate the issue of securities, thus removing the states from this area. The commission was to regulate consolidation in such a way that competition would be preserved. The ICC also was given much greater authority in the venue of service. It could order lines extended, unify roads in emergencies, supervise car distribution, and supervise joint terminal use and use of safety appliances.[39]

The act created the United States Railroad Labor Board (RLB), which was given both mediation and arbitration authority over disputes. Management, labor, and the public were each to be represented by three members on the RLB, who were to be appointed by the president. The RLB had jurisdiction over grievances and questions of rules and working conditions that could not be settled by local boards of adjustment, and it could suspend wage increases in certain situations. Strikes were not outlawed. Unlike the boards of adjustment under the USRA, the new boards were voluntary, which immediately weakened the RLB. A second, more important flaw was that the RLB had no power to enforce its rulings.[40]

Although the new law drew labor's ire, it was in many respects a continuation of progressive policies. Like pre-war and wartime policy, the Transportation Act attempted to promote the public good through creating—the framers hoped—an efficient railway system. Like pre-war railroad policy, but not that of wartime, the federal government no longer guaranteed union organization. From labor's perspective, one of the principal problems of pre-war railroad labor legislation was its voluntary nature. The Transportation Act, like its pre-war antecedents, placed unions essentially at the mercy of the carriers. It is also noteworthy that in the politically charged atmosphere of the post-war Red Scare the GOP-sponsored Transportation Act limited corporate profits and partially restricted management prerogatives.

Unions were unhappy with the Transportation Act. The *BLE Journal* editorialized that the only feature of the act that showed any consideration for employees was the clause that protected wages from reductions until September 1, 1920. It called the Transportation Act "vicious" and "a rank piece of legislation." Labor turned to what it believed was its best weapon—the ballot box—and began to mobilize for the fall election. Its ultimate goal was to substitute a new law for the Transportation Act, one that "will be more in keeping with the principles of Democracy for which our American boys gave up their lives in the Great World War."[41] Railroad labor editors were not afraid to draw on the wartime rhetoric of industrial democracy. With the elections approaching, railroad labor quickly turned to the ballot box to assert their rights.

Conclusion

Although the railroad unions were unsuccessful in enacting the Plumb Plan or stopping the Transportation Act from becoming law, they laid important groundwork for their own political future. Cooperation in the Plumb Plan League, creation of *Labor*, and the call to political arms in the 1920 elections were new to the operating brotherhoods. In June 1920 the *BLEJ* told its readers that labor had for too long kept in the background " . . . because it was afraid of the political scarecrow, but we are now boldly entering the legislative field."[42] Only three years earlier the *Journal* had reminded its readers that it was against the union's law to discuss politics with other members.[43] However, railroad labor wanted a voice in the industry and was applying the lessons of industrial democracy. For them, the war was in some respects just beginning as the election of 1920 drew nearer.

· 4 ·

Grassroots Political Organization

The election of 1920 was a reversal of traditional political strategy for railroad unions. While they had engaged in lobbying, they had generally remained outside the fray of partisan politics. As recently as 1917, the *BLEJ* had urged engineers not to discuss politics in division rooms.[1] The brotherhoods had broken with tradition in 1916 by endorsing President Wilson. While significant, it was not a harbinger of systemic change. The Democrats counted on labor support in 1918, but the unions, aside from urging members to vote, did little.

Railroaders changed their political policy because their wartime gains were in jeopardy. Their goal was to elect enough pro-labor legislators to amend Title III of the Transportation Act, which created the RLB. Warren S. Stone, Grand Chief Engineer of the BLE, reminded members in the spring of 1920 that they were entering the " . . . most critical time ever for organized labor. The time has arrived when we should reward our friends and defeat our enemies."[2] The AFL endorsed the same policy for years, but gravitated to the Democratic party during the Wilson administration. By the end of the war, the AFL retreated to a less active political stance, opening the way for railroad labor unions to assume the leadership role.

Union Criticism of the Transportation Act

The *BLEJ* claimed that the RLB had three critical weaknesses. First, it was not impartial. Second, the railroads would enlist the help of the courts if labor did not obey rulings. Finally, subordinate officials and union members were represented by the same men.[3] Subordinate officials held low-level management positions. Some were union members who had been promoted, and others were hired directly to their positions. The board's greatest weakness, however, proved to be its lack of enforcement authority. Eventually, both sides ignored its rulings with no fear of negative consequences.

Another weakness was that the law did not require that the three National Boards of Adjustment that had functioned under the USRA be maintained. It made the boards voluntary, and labor was eager to reestablish them. Executives were keen to reestablish local control, while unions wanted to maintain the uniformity and standardization that they had gained during the war.[4] E. E. Loomis, president of the Lehigh Valley Railroad, summed up the opinion of management: "I do not think I need to burden you with discussion of the evils of standardization . . . centralization . . . may have been necessary when our country was at war. It is not necessary today."[5] Because few voluntary boards were established, the RLB heard numerous minor cases, which could have been solved locally.[6]

In 1920, with the Esch-Cummins Bill about to become law, union executives decided to keep the Plumb Plan League and *Labor* operating.[7] Although *Labor* had been published less than a year, its wide circulation and growing influence were readily apparent. One illustration of *Labor*'s impact occurred when representatives John Cooper and Israel Foster, both of Ohio, complained in a letter to the editor about its cartoons and editorials. Cooper wrote that *Labor* "poisoned the minds of men." His complaint stemmed from letters to the paper written by several of his constituents, blasting his voting record. Both representatives suggested that fellow congressman J. M. Baer (R-ND), who drew many of the newspaper's cartoons, should resign from the House.[8] Although he did not resign, he did not win reelection in 1920.

The Elections of 1920

Unions were under siege by the summer of 1920. Strikes in Seattle, by Boston police, and against the giant U.S. Steel Corporation, all in 1919, made national headlines, and in each case labor lost. These strikes were just the tip of the iceberg, as thousands of workers struck in the months after the war. Prompted by their precarious position and the wartime rhetoric of democracy, labor organizations turned to the ballot box.

The best way for workers to show their strength and frustration was to vote en masse. The railroad unions used the six hundred branches of the Plumb Plan League to get their message to members. As the election neared, union publications urged men to discuss candidates and issues at union meetings, to register themselves and their families to vote, and to become active in primary campaigns. Additionally, the AFL sent requests to forty thousand locals asking them to appoint an election committee.[9] Labor's nonpartisan campaign reached all thirty-two states in which a Senate seat was being contested.[10]

In the election of 1920, the outline of what historian Erik Olssen called railroad labor's political machine first became apparent. The brotherhoods used *Labor* and their monthly magazines to support their political agenda. They published special editions of *Labor* to support their friends. Unions also directed their organizers and lobbyists to mobilize the rank and file behind favored candidates. As their political organization grew in sophistication, the executives formed a committee that examined politicians' records and disseminated the information to the membership.[11]

The goal of the union coalition was to defeat all Transportation Act supporters, but the principal targets were Esch and Cummins. Labor's first important test came in the Iowa primaries in June, where Cummins faced Smith Wildman Brookhart in the Republican Party primary. On the Saturday before the election, union members distributed literature all over the Hawkeye State. Thousands of cards were distributed instructing voters on how to change their party affiliation and how to take out absentee ballots. In addition to opposing the Transportation Act, Brookhart's platform supported cooperative marketing for farmers, the Rochdale system, a comprehensive social insurance scheme, and a soldier's bonus to be paid for by taxing war profits.[12] After a slow start, Cummins rallied and won the primary by 20,000 votes out of 215,000 votes cast.[13] On the surface the contest was not close, but it suggests growing discontent among voters, which Brookhart's supporters exploited. It also indicates the growing political organization of the railroad labor alliance. Union publications crowed about Brookhart's strong challenge in the primary.

Esch did not fare as well. An eleven-term incumbent from western Wisconsin, Esch lost in the GOP primary to Joseph Beck, who went on to win the general election and served in Congress until 1929. As in Iowa, railroaders registered voters and distributed campaign literature. All Wisconsin voters seem to have rallied around the Transportation Act issue because only one Wisconsin legislator who voted for the Esch-Cummins Bill, Senator Irvine Lenroot, won in the primaries. He won because two progressives split the vote.[14] Clearly, the state's powerful progressive forces, led by Republican Senator Robert La Follette, were hard at work.

There were other significant issues in the Wisconsin election, but railroad labor was quick to take credit for the victories. A RED circular letter trumpeted Esch's defeat and called the Transportation Act " . . . that infamous, obnoxious, anti-labor bill which affected the interest of every railway employe [*sic*] in the country. This shows what we can do when we drop out of partisan politics and go to the polls and vote against our enemies and vote for our friends."[15]

Labor reported that because of primary losses, openings had been created in several important committees in the House, including the House Interstate and Foreign Commerce Committee. *Labor* claimed that in addition to Esch, vice chairman Edward L. Hamilton (R-MI), and Arthur G. De Walt (D-PA) suffered primary defeats. In truth, both men retired, while in the Senate, Transportation Act supporters Hoke Smith (D-GA), Charles S. Thomas (D-CO), and Lawrence Y. Sherman (R-IL) lost primary races.[16] Regardless of circumstances, *Labor* considered the loss of Transportation Act supporters a victory and was quick to give credit for those defeats to union-organized voters.

While the congressional races offered labor a chance for success, the presidential race did not. The Republicans nominated Ohio's Senator Warren G. Harding and the Democrats nominated Ohio Governor James Cox. A party stalwart, Harding supported the Transportation Act. Harding's nomination prompted Senator La Follette to begin organizing a third party campaign. In a letter to President William H. Johnston of the International Association of Machinists, he referred to the just-concluded Republican convention as the " . . . house of the dead." He continued, "The Republican party, as a party, has learned nothing in thirty years . . . and I am confident if the shade of 1888 could be brought back and thrust into the present situation that shade would have a more comprehensive grasp of present day problems than has or is possible of the 1920 candidate." The drift away from progressive ideals alarmed La Follette, and he wrote that only a new party could solve the nation's problems.[17] Although Cox had a solid pro-labor voting record, the unions were never very excited about his candidacy.[18]

Although there was support for a third party in some quarters, most railroad union leaders opposed the idea.[19] The AFL also resisted a third party, believing it would only hurt their efforts and draw votes from progressives of the traditional parties. Union opposition was critical, and a key factor in La Follette's decision not to run.

Labor leaders considered their nonpartisan campaign of 1920 quite successful. Labor reelected every member of the House of Representatives with a perfect record on labor issues, and at least fifty who were considered inconsiderate or hostile lost. Labor publications seldom mentioned the labor views of winners. Gompers, trying to put the best spin on the elections, estimated that fifty-five to sixty representatives whose records showed fair to considerate service were elected. Labor leaders had to emphasize their success at the polls, no matter how dubious, to keep the rank and file politically motivated. Harding defeated Cox by approximately seven million votes, and his long coattails gave the GOP a 309–132 majority in the House and a 59–37 margin in the Senate.[20]

Political Alliances

Progressives rallied in the aftermath of the election in an attempt to focus the national political debate on issues they felt were important. The nominal leader of the progressive forces, Senator La Follette, known by the sobriquet "Battling Bob," was not going to quit. He created the Peoples Legislative Service to compile facts for members of Congress, to analyze those facts, and to inform the people about impending legislation.[21] The AFL was also apparently trying to reinvigorate its political activities, because on April 12, 1921, railroad labor executives and representatives of the AFL met to discuss forming a political alliance. Gompers proposed establishing a permanent steering committee to handle legislative issues. Each of the three groups of railroad employees would have one representative, and the AFL would appoint three members. The operating brotherhoods opposed the idea. L. E. Sheppard, president of the ORC writing for the brotherhoods, stated in a letter to Bert M. Jewell, president of the RED:

> We feel that we would not, in the future, receive the consideration we believe we have a right to expect and, holding the view that the Railroad Groups should be privileged to outline a policy in all railroad matters and with past experience staring us in the face (notwithstanding the present assurances that we would have autonomy in these matters), we have decided that it would be wiser to refrain from going through with this contemplated alliance.[22]

The AFL-proposed alliance failed to materialize. However, the following year the operating brotherhoods, along with the RED, forged their own coalition, the Railroad Labor Executives Association (RLEA), to facilitate greater political cooperation. President Johnston of the IAM suggested a more formal union alliance. Johnston was more militant than most of his peers in the AFL; he supported industrial unionism, nonpartisan political activities, and government intervention in the economy. His opposition to the AFL's "pure and simple" unionism may have been as a result of his early years as a member of the Knights of Labor. Johnston, born in Canada in 1874, moved to Rhode Island as a child and entered the trade at the age of twenty. He joined the IAM in 1895 and immediately became active in his local union. He worked his way up through the IAM hierarchy, becoming its president in 1911—a position he held until his resignation in 1926.

In December 1921 Johnston wrote Jewell, urging him to call a meeting of the sixteen standard organizations " . . . for the purpose of considering the Plumb Plan and other matters of mutual interest." Johnston noted that no one within the labor movement had the authority to approach Congress on behalf of the entire movement. He wanted the labor leaders to consider political action in the upcoming (1922) elections.[23] Early in 1922, labor leaders founded the RLEA. While the RLEA embraced Johnston's arguments for increased political activity, it dismissed his more radical ideas concerning government ownership of the railroads and other quasi-public enterprises.

Formation of the RLEA was the capstone of a gradual movement toward interunion cooperation. With the railroad unions mobilized, Johnston urged his peers to form a broader alliance. He argued that a " . . . coalition of all progressive forces including the minority parties, the labor unions, and other liberal groups" should be established. He hoped the coalition could agree on a few basic principles, such as public ownership of railroads, telegraphs, and telephones and the fundamental rights as guaranteed in the first amendment.[24] Johnston was one of the few railroad union presidents who favored the formation of a third party. Most of his platform was too radical for other labor leaders, but they agreed that a broader, more cohesive political alliance was necessary.

On February 11, 1922, shortly after the RLEA's founding, *Labor* announced that progressive groups would confer in Chicago on Washington's birthday—February 22—to bring together constructive forces already in existence, but not to form a third party.[25] At the convention, railroad labor executives and

HIS STANDARD BEARER

Drawn for LABOR by John M. Baer

GOVERNMENT OF THE PEOPLE, BY THE PEOPLE, AND FOR THE PEOPLE, SHALL NOT PERISH FROM THE EARTH

Figure 4. Union leaders frequently sought to link their activities to patriotic symbols. In this illustration, presidential hopeful Robert M. La Follette accepts the banner from an iconic figure of Abraham Lincoln.

their political allies established the Conference for Progressive Political Action (CPPA), which the brotherhoods structured so that control rested firmly with them. Johnston and other more radical leaders favored a third party, but the majority of their peers did not.

Because of the diverse nature of the CPPA, it would have been impossible to agree on a platform. Building on the nonpartisan foundation of 1920 allowed the CPPA to delay the sticky platform issue.[26] The CPPA elected to work through established nonpartisan organizations, such as the Non-Partisan League, labor unions, and agricultural groups. A nonpartisan approach also gave progressives a better opportunity to build on their previous successes. The regular party politicians were most vulnerable to grassroots political action in the primaries, so that is where the CPPA focused its energy.[27] It is impossible to determine what chilling effect, if any, the Red Scare had on the decisions of the CPPA, but certainly one must consider its influence.

The statement of principles issued by the delegates confirmed their faith in American democracy, but lamented that it had been usurped by plutocracy and privilege. The delegates endorsed three resolutions. The first called for progressives to form local committees to back candidates " . . . who are pledged to the interests of the producing classes and to the principles of genuine democracy in agriculture, industry, and government." The second resolution called for a Committee of Fifteen to coordinate the local committees' activities. The final resolution pledged the financial support of the organizations involved for the Committee of Fifteen.[28]

The AFL leadership was not represented at the meeting. Gompers declined an invitation, which is curious since earlier he suggested an "offensive and defensive" political alliance between the rail unions and the AFL. The failure of the brotherhoods and the AFL to come together seems to lie in the relationship between Stone and Gompers, who were suspicious of each other. Neither man wanted to appear to be subordinate to the other. The AFL Executive Council decided that it should participate in the upcoming primaries, but in cooperation with the CPPA.[29]

Labor Unrest and the Shopmen's Strike

Americans entered the post-war years with optimism. Industrial workers hoped that the war was the talisman of a brighter future. The wartime rhetoric of democracy, freedom, and industrial democracy were enthusiastically embraced by workers.[30] Their bosses, however, had a much different vision of the post-war world. The labor question, according to President Wilson, writing in 1919,

> stands at the front of all others amidst the present great awakening . . . The object of all reform in this essential matter must be the genuine democratization of industry, based upon a full recognition of the right of those who work, in whatever rank to participate in the some organic way in every decision which directly affects their welfare.[31]

In 1919, the greatest strike wave in American history swept the nation. Historian Melvyn Dubofsky writes that 1919 was like no other year in American history. David Montgomery notes that "the phrase 'workers' control,' seldom heard before that time, became a popular catchword throughout the labor movement."[32] As wartime labor agreements expired and federal protection disappeared, industrialists vigorously reasserted their authority. There were more than three thousand strikes involving more than four million workers, or 22 percent of the total workforce.[33] Fear swept the nation as May 1, 1920, approached. Although one person died and forty were injured in May Day riots in Cleveland, the worst of the Red Scare was over by the summer of 1920.[34]

Because of the commercial disruption and likely accompanying violence, the specter of a nationwide railroad strike hung over the nation. The various federal laws that had governed railroad labor relations since the late 1880s had averted a national rail strike since the Pullman strike of 1894. Rail unionists had benefited from wartime mobilization, but the carriers felt particularly maligned. All parties hoped that the Transportation Act of 1920 would solve the labor question; it did not. Unions used the fear of a disruptive strike to their advantage.

In the fall of 1920, the Association of Railway Executives (ARE), keen to eliminate all remnants of federal control, stepped up its efforts to reassert managerial authority. W. W. Atterbury, vice president of the Pennsylvania Railroad and chairman of the ARE's labor committee, was a formidable opponent. After graduation from Yale in 1886 he went to work for the Pennsylvania Railroad and rose steadily to become a vice president in 1909. He handled transportation for the U.S. Army in 1916 when it fought Pancho Villa. During World War I he was commissioned a brigadier general and appointed director general for the American Expeditionary Force in France. As the ARE point man, he announced that the carriers wanted to reestablish the pre-war system of labor relations.[35] In early 1921, claiming impending financial ruin, the ARE asked the RLB to terminate USRA national agreements and work rules, which it claimed would cut annual expenses by at least $300 million.[36]

Union leaders believed that the railroads were trying to take advantage of the economic crisis to slash wages. In a telegram to President Wilson, labor executives demanded that the carriers present evidence to support their financial claims. The union leaders argued the ARE's statement was hyperbole intended to gain public sympathy.[37] The carriers argued that slashing wages would allow them to cut rates.

Prompting the carriers' request was the sharp economic decline that began in the middle of 1920, shortly after railway workers' last wage increase. By the end of the year, thousands of Americans were out of work; nationally unemployment was approximately 12 percent. Railroad employment fell from nearly 2.2 million in August 1920 to approximately 1.6 million the following March, a 27 percent decline.[38] Farm prices also declined dramatically.

The RLB heard the carriers' request to reduce wages in April 1921. The companies presented data compiled by the Chicago Great Western Railroad to illustrate their woes. The carrier showed that while it was paying fifty-five cents an hour for unskilled labor, thirty-seven industries along its lines were paying forty-three cents an hour. Similarly, it paid an average of eighty-five cents an hour to machinists and other mechanical employees, while ninety-three industries along its lines paid an average of sixty-three cents an hour for comparable work.[39]

Decision No. 147 of the RLB, issued on July 1, 1921, reduced wages an average of 12 percent for " . . . practically all of the large carriers and all classes of employees." Those at the bottom of the pay scale saw their wages reduced the most. *Railway Age* estimated that the decision would reduce the carriers' annual payroll by $400 million.[40] Although railroad workers may have felt singled out, many American workers experienced wage cuts, and farmers suffered a dramatic drop in agricultural prices.

Railroaders were growing increasingly frustrated. In the late spring and early summer of 1921 talk of a strike was rife, but the brotherhoods opposed the idea, so it gained little traction.[41] In the fall, tensions rose again because executives requested a 10 percent wage reduction.[42] Decision 119, which terminated the wartime national agreements, also angered labor. Further, labor believed that President Harding violated the spirit, if not the letter, of the law when he appointed W. L. McMeninen to replace J. J. Forrester as a labor representative on the RLB. McMeninen did not have the support of his union, the trainmen.[43] Labor was more upset, however, because the board condemned with far more vigor labor violations of its rulings than carrier noncompliance.[44]

Immediately after the carriers' request, labor leaders acted. The four operating unions and SUNA requested a conference with the carriers, who refused. Union members voted to strike on October 30. Three-quarters of a million railroaders were ready to walk out immediately, and more than 1.2 million were set to follow over the next several weeks. The unions planned to strike different lines at various times over a period of days.[45]

The possibility of a national strike was cause for great concern. On October 16, 1921, the *New York Times* ran a headline across its front page proclaiming the possibility of a national railroad strike that might precipitate food rationing. Senator Albert Cummins (R-IA), chief architect of the Transportation Act of 1920, which created the RLB, captured the sentiment of much of the general public and railroad management:

> If there is a railroad strike it will prove an unspeakable disaster. Its effects on business conditions, on the country generally, is [*sic*] horrible even to contemplate. It would add materially to the difficulties already presented.[46]

Cummins identified the second major issue at stake: the validity and credibility of the RLB. The dispute, he said, should be settled by the RLB. Cutting to the heart of the issue Cummins argued, "Of course, if both sides are not willing to permit arbitration by the RLB of their differences, then the Railroad Act becomes entirely ineffective."[47]

The RLB called a meeting of representatives of both parties. The *Times* noted it " . . . was the first step to determine whether the board was in fact a 'futile' agency." A strike, the *Times* reported, based on the refusal to accept a ruling of the RLB would be a blow to society " . . . which the government cannot disregard."[48] If the RLB were to become a "futile" agency, there was a distinct possibility that the nation's railroads would be thrown into chaos. Railroad presidents were adamant in their opinion that the potential strike was a threat to the legitimacy of the RLB, and by extension the entire government. Some believed that the threat of a strike was an attempt to bring about government control.[49]

Attorney General Harry M. Daugherty said that the government would concede that the men had the right to walk out, but noted that striking in scattered groups, as the unions proposed, might be a violation of federal conspiracy law. Given the events the following year during the shopmen's strike, he said, prophetically:

The Government has the power and ample authority, and it will be as just and reasonable as it can be, but these arteries of commerce must continue to serve the people, property must be preserved, life protected, law enforced and order maintained. The Government is big enough and strong enough to see that this is accomplished.[50]

One reason the unions ultimately did not strike was that public opinion was largely against them. Typical of public response to the potential strike is D. B. Ryland, who wrote to Secretary of Commerce Herbert Hoover, " . . . our entire business interests and public are solidly behind no compromise with the organized labor as represented by the several railway unions." Further, he wrote that it is " . . . crass effrontery" for the unions to seek special legislation.[51]

The RLB conference succeeded. The board stated that the strike " . . . would have resulted in a national calamity of incalculable magnitude." Further, calling a strike in protest against Decision 147, which reduced wages, would be a violation of the Transportation Act. The board congratulated the carriers and unions " . . . on this return to industrial peace, triumph of the reign of law, and the escape from this national disaster." The board's decision ended with a cautionary note to both carriers and unions " . . . either party tending to and threatening an interruption of the transportation lines . . . are in themselves, even when they do not culminate in a stoppage of traffic, a cause and source of great injury and damage."[52] In addition, the RLB assured unions that it would not take up the request for further wage reductions until it had ruled on other questions dealing with the roads' return to private operation, which would take a considerable amount of time.[53]

Railway Age contended that the unions were prepared for an extended strike and that, because the RLB caseload was so heavy, it would not rule on the complaint for several months.[54] *Railway Age* identified a crucial weakness of the RLB—its heavy caseload. Because the carriers and unions could not agree on establishing boards of adjustment, the RLB received many cases that could have been handled locally. In the six years the RLB operated, it disposed of 13,169 cases of which 6,195 were local in nature, often involving one or two employees.[55]

Termination of the national agreements and wage cuts set the stage for the national shopmen's strike. Shopmen were among the major beneficiaries of federal control and believed that the wage cut undermined nearly every benefit they had gained under federal control. Jewell said that the wage cut was a setback and that it eliminated every complaint that the carriers had against the National Agreements.[56]

The inability of the RLB to enforce its rulings created tension that mounted as other companies followed the example of the Pennsylvania and Erie railroads; both stated that they would ignore RLB rulings that they did not like.[57] The refusal of some carriers to abide by RLB rulings was a severe blow to unions and the prestige of the RLB. In addition to wage cuts, many carriers began to contract work to independent machine shops to further reduce costs. The RLB ordered the roads to discontinue this practice, but they continued it anyway.[58] Joseph Beck, whom the railroaders had helped to defeat Esch in 1920, introduced legislation that would have required carriers to get ICC approval before outsourcing equipment repairs.[59] All these developments alarmed the craft unions.

The tense situation reached its breaking point when the carriers requested another wage reduction. The unions countered by demanding a wage increase, arguing that many workers could scarcely survive on their current wages. The RLB ruled in March 1922 that, effective on July 1, the wages of maintenance of way employees, shopcraft workers, clerical and station employees, stationary engine and boiler room employees, and signal department workers would be reduced—some by as much as 20 percent.[60]

The decision was virtually a declaration of war. President Johnston of the Machinists summed up his union's complaints in a letter to President Warren G. Harding. He told the president that ninety-two railroads had violated the Transportation Act or a RLB decision in 104 cases involving work normally done by the shop crafts, wage decisions, interpretations of rules, and the right of employees to choose their own representatives. Further, the RLB abolished overtime pay for Sundays and holidays, which workers had enjoyed for thirty years. Johnston was also angry because the Pennsylvania Railroad refused to comply with an RLB decision after a federal judge ruled that its decisions on wages and rules were only advisory.[61]

On Saturday, July 1, 1922, just over 256,000—or about 75 percent—of the nation's shopmen went on strike. In many localities the strikers met immediately after they left work to choose local leaders. Guidelines for choosing the local strike committees were specified in an RED circular on June 27. Strikers were also reminded not to engage in illegal activities.[62] President Harding publicly supported the RLB, but was also distressed at the carriers' willingness to flaunt the board's rulings.[63] The RLB responded two days later. Chairman Ben Hooper introduced a resolution, which passed by a 5–2 vote and declared the strike illegal, that the strikers had no claims to the jobs that they had left voluntarily, that the replacement workers were not strikebreakers, but were fulfilling a moral obligation, and that the strikers were breaking the law.[64] Jewell charged, "The history of the recent conduct of the board is a history of repeated injustices and usurpations all having as the indirect object the establishment of tyranny over the workers engaged in the transportation industry."[65]

The strike, and the violence that accompanied it, threatened both the national economy and civil order in many cities. The carriers hired thousands of extra guards. At one extreme was the Pennsylvania Railroad, which hired 16,215 guards and had a striker–to-guard ratio of 1:1.5, and on the other end of the spectrum was the Chicago and Alton Railroad, which hired 130 guards and had a striker to guard ratio of 1:18.[66] It did not take long for violence to occur. At least nine people were killed by railroad guards between July 8 and 20, including three children. Strikers also resorted to acts of violence. In Oroville, CA, about seventy-five masked men attacked guards and strikebreakers at the Western Pacific roundhouse, causing numerous injuries, one perhaps fatal. Additionally, four men were missing and presumed kidnapped. In other locations, strikers persuaded their replacements to lay down their tools.[67]

Some carriers cancelled scheduled service, and in Texas eighteen thousand troops were ordered to be ready for instant entrainment. In New Jersey an extra fifty federal deputies were sworn in to protect U.S. Mail trains moving through the state, although no threats to the trains had been made. According to state authorities, Attorney General Daugherty had authorized the hiring of as many as five hundred extra marshals.

The president's cabinet was divided. One faction, led by Daugherty, wanted to break the strike, while Secretary of Commerce Herbert Hoover and Secretary of Labor James Davis sought a compromise.[68] The deadlock continued until September 1 when, acting on the president's order, Daugherty—who believed the strike was part of communist plot—persuaded Federal District Judge James Wilkerson to issue an injunction, which was one of the broadest ever issued against labor. Historian Irving Bernstein called it majestic "for the dazzling number and variety of prohibited acts." Wilkerson, citing the Sherman Anti-Trust Act, the Debs ruling of 1894, and every other anti-labor ruling from the Supreme Court since 1894, forbade every written, oral, and physical act in furtherance of the criminal act that was the strike. Wilkerson believed the strikers had engaged in a widespread conspiracy to interrupt commerce and intimidate strikebreakers.[69]

The Election of 1922

The defeat solidified labor's desire to eliminate the RLB.[70] As tensions mounted in the spring, Stone urged engineers to vote, calling it a matter of self-preservation.[71] In May, he addressed the BLFE convention and asked them to become more politically active. He warned them that they should not expect the 253 lawyers in Congress to do anything that would benefit labor.[72] No doubt many unionists agreed with William G. McAdoo, who wrote to a friend during the strike, "Certainly the President and Congress are cutting a pitiable figure before the country."[73]

The strike defeat was a clarion call to elect less pitiable figures. To that end, the BLFE, the ORC, and the Brotherhood of Railway and Steamship Clerks, Freight Handlers, Express and Station Employees all voted to buy each member a subscription to *Labor*, which increased the paper's circulation to nearly half a million. Readers were exhorted to be like missionaries and " . . . spread the gospel."[74]

Labor waged an aggressive campaign using the shopmen's injunction as its main rallying point.[75] For the first time, *Labor* issued special editions endorsing candidates. On November 7, 1922, Republicans suffered losses at the state and national levels. *Labor* optimistically reported that the administration's victory two years earlier " . . . was repudiated by a smashing majority in a sufficient number of states to have decided a presidential election."[76] Sixteen of labor's twenty endorsed candidates for the U.S. Senate won, which helped to cut the GOP majority in the Senate from twenty-two to eleven. Among the new progressive members of the Senate were Henrik Shipstead, (Farm-Labor MN), Lynn Frazier, (R-ND), Smith Brookhart (R-IA), and Robert Howell (R-NB). La Follette's victory—he garnered 82 percent of the vote—was especially significant to railroaders because he was their champion. He insisted that railroad unions were crucial to his victory.[77]

The labor press argued that the GOP losses reversed the political road taken in 1920. The results for the House, where the GOP majority dropped from 170 to 20, were also encouraging. Ninety-three undesirable congressmen lost, and leaders of the CPPA estimated that 140 congressmen were "progressive minded." Although the "progressive minded" were still a minority, in a House often divided over issues that cut across party lines, they could have significant influence. The success of labor-supported candidates in Midwestern states reflects, at least in part, the close ties that labor and agriculture established after 1920.[78]

The labor movement's assessment of the elections was perhaps overly optimistic because it considered the loss of any anti-labor politician a victory. They often chose to ignore the record of the incoming legislator. La Follette's victory encouraged him to revive his presidential hopes, and he believed that the elections had halted the great drive to create industrial serfdom in America. In the fall of 1922, La Follette wrote, "I believe that we have reached a point where the organization of a well-defined group can be consummated." Many progressives—but not most labor executives—hoped that the CPPA would spawn a third party.[79]

The CPPA met in December, and the third party question divided the convention. Socialists and intellectuals generally favored a third party, while most trade unionists preferred a nonpartisan approach. The voting procedures favored the more conservative faction led by the railroad unions; the resolution to form a third party lost by a vote of 64–52. A second issue before the CPPA was its support of a motion made by Edward Keating, the editor of *Labor*, to deny the communist delegates' credentials.[80] Rejecting the communists was crucial if the group hoped to gain support among the more conservative members of the labor movement and the general public.

Agreeing on a platform was difficult. Socialists wanted an agenda that included statements concerning child labor, public ownership of power, war, imperialism, and nationalization of coal mines. Those who favored the nonpartisan approach wanted a more ambiguous platform. Keating, who served as Chairman of the Resolutions Committee, submitted a brief, six-point platform that was vague enough that politicians would not be tainted by the CPPA's endorsement. The platform reflected Keating's early political influences. It addressed problems that populists and progressives had been trying to solve for more than thirty years; some parts of it were reminiscent of the Omaha Platform of 1892. The key points endorsed the repeal of the Transportation Act, public ownership of coal mines, water power and hydro-electric power, the direct election of the president and vice president, and the extension of direct primary laws. To appeal to the farm bloc it also endorsed the Norris-Sinclair Consumers and Producers Financing Corporation Bill, designed to increase farm prices and reduce the cost for agricultural products, and to create an independent system of food producers' credits.[81]

While the CPPA endorsed the "post card platform," the railroad unions remained unconvinced. The primary objective of the unions was to abolish the RLB, not to advance the CPPA's broader agenda. Even on the issue of the RLB, the unions did not devise a single response. Various statements appeared in the November and December 1922 issues of the *Engineers Journal*, which illustrated their lack of a defined program. In November a cartoon appeared in the *Journal* depicting Uncle Sam looking out over a troubled railroad yard. In his hand he held a copy of the Plumb Plan, and he said, "Plumb was right."[82] The following month, in a discussion of the upcoming CPPA convention, the *Journal* wrote, "No definite plan [concerning the railroads] has been announced, but it will probably repeal the Esch-Cummins Act."

Conclusion

Since the end of the Great War, organized labor had suffered tremendous setbacks. Hundreds of strikes had ended in defeat, and organized labor, at least one segment of it, had taken action. The rhetoric of industrial democracy, so prominent during the war, had not wholly disappeared. By the end of 1922, the railroad unions had taken great strides toward becoming more politically active, but had avoided forming a third party. They had established the Railroad Labor Executives Association to coordinate their legislative activity and the Conference for Progressive Political Action to apply greater pressure on Congress, but their primary objective was still to overthrow Title III of the Transportation Act. By taking such a leadership position in these two organizations, the railroad brotherhoods had supplanted the American Federation of Labor as the leading voice of American labor. In 1923 the unions began to vigorously work with their congressional allies to amend the Transportation Act and abolish the now-hated Railroad Labor Board.

· 5 ·

The Road to Political Power, 1922–1924

The fight to abolish the RLB occurred in two stages. The first stage began after the shopmen's strike of 1922 and ended with the election of Calvin Coolidge in 1924. Until the shopmen's strike, railroad operatives took a wait-and-see approach toward the RLB, but the strike convinced them that they had to act and eliminate it. Although the war had been over for more than four years, labor clung to its belief in the power of industrial democracy and the ballot box. The threat of another national strike was also a potent weapon for the unions.

Between the strike and the election of 1924, the unions made progress toward their goal. The RLEA spent 1923 writing legislation that Representative Alben Barkley (D-KY) and Senator Robert Howell (R-NB) introduced in February 1924. Further, President Coolidge told Congress in his annual message of 1923 that the current situation on the railroads was " . . . not entirely satisfactory."[1] The efforts of labor to write legislation and the threat of national strikes convinced the Republican leadership that the demands of railroad labor could no longer be ignored.[2] Although traffic declined, the carriers kept trains running during the shopmen's strike, but it would have been nearly impossible for the railroads to operate without engineers, firemen, conductors, and trainmen.[3]

After the elections of 1922, the unions moved quickly to abolish the RLB. The day after the midterms Bert M. Jewell, president of the RED, urged Warren Stone of the BLE to take a leading role in the effort to repeal the Transportation Act.[4] A committee of union leaders, charged with drafting labor amendments to the Transportation Act, met in January 1923. Even before being officially given the task, Donald Richberg—the union's general counsel who had replaced Glenn Plumb when he died—and his associate David E. Lilienthal had begun to work on the proposal.[5]

Richberg's view of the relationship between labor and capital was critical in shaping the legislation; like many progressives he believed that the employing classes wielded coercive power over laboring men and women. The legislation had to create a more equitable relationship between railroad workers and their employers. As with earlier legislation, the ultimate goal was to prevent crippling strikes.[6]

A year later, Richberg and Lilienthal had a proposal prepared for the RLEA to submit to their congressional allies, namely Barkley and Howell. The authors assumed that all Americans wanted continuity, safety, and efficiency in their railroad network. According to Lilienthal, "honest collective bargaining" was the dominating principle of the bill. He was also insistent that the public representatives be removed from the dispute resolution process. His position challenged the system, which had long been based on a tripartite model in which labor, management, and the public were represented equally on resolution boards. Lilienthal wrote that the doctrine of a public member was fine-sounding, but was really " . . . quackery of the cheapest sort." He argued that railroaders themselves should solve labor disputes.[7]

The proposal replaced the RLB with machinery for direct mediation and voluntary arbitration, which would be carried out by the unions. Other key provisions allowed all employees to maintain their unions and to choose their own representatives to negotiate with carriers, and it created National Boards of Adjustment. The Howell-Barkley Bill made it the duty of both parties to " . . . exert every reasonable effort to make and maintain agreements" concerning wages and working conditions. Such conferences were long the practice in the industry, and transforming them into a legal obligation, Lilienthal wrote, was a short step.[8] The proposal specified that no changes in working conditions or rules could be made without following the procedure outlined in the bill. Disputes not settled in local conferences were to be submitted to one of the four Boards of Adjustment. Carriers and employees would be equally represented on the boards.

If the Boards of Adjustment failed, the conflict would be submitted to Boards of Mediation and Conciliation. A third tier of dispute resolution machinery, the Board of Arbitration, was the final step in the process. Both parties had to agree to accept the Board's decision before submitting the dispute. The proposal called for the carriers and unions each to appoint one-third

Figure 5. David B. Robertson, BLFE president and leader of the RLEA. By permission of the United Transportation Union.

of members to the Board of Arbitration, who were to name the remaining board members. The bill required the Board to submit all decisions to the federal courts, and if neither side objected within ten days, it would be entered as a court judgment.[9] A weakness in previous legislation was that decisions were always voluntary, thus giving rulings the force of the courts would have been an important victory for labor. By the middle of the decade, carriers, most notably the Pennsylvania and the Erie, routinely ignored the RLB.

The union bill dealt solely with the labor section of the Transportation Act. David B. Robertson, president of the BLFE and chairman of the RLEA special committee, charged with drafting the bill, told a Senate subcommittee that the proposed legislation was an industrial code made up from the written and unwritten laws that governed labor relations on the railroads for many years. It took the outstanding features of the Erdman Act of 1898 and the Newlands Act of 1913, and synthesized them into a new bill.[10]

Robertson was an important leader of the railroad unions who emerged after Stone's death. He served as president of the BLFE until 1953. The Ohio native began working for the Pennsylvania Railroad as a wiper in 1895. In 1898, he began working for the Erie Railroad as hostler, fireman, and engineer. The union members elected him general chairman of the BLFE on the Erie in 1905, vice president of the BLFE in 1913, and president in 1922. He was instrumental in the passage of the Railway Labor Act and served as chair of the RLEA from 1926–1932.[11]

The need to address the labor question increased during the year that Richberg and Lilienthal worked to draft the bill. As they labored, the United States Supreme Court issued a ruling that further weakened the RLB. Chief Justice William Howard Taft, writing for the majority, upheld a lower court's ruling that Congress failed to grant the RLB sufficient power to enforce its decisions. Its only enforcement mechanism was the power of public opinion.[12] The case before the court began with the refusal of the Pennsylvania Railroad to meet with representatives of the shopcraft union, System Federation No. 90, which belonged to the RED. The controversy began when the wartime national agreements expired and questions arose over wages and work rules. The carrier said it would only meet with representatives from the company-sponsored union.[13] This ruling, along with the carriers' history of ignoring RLB rulings, surely influenced Richberg and Lilienthal to include an enforcement mechanism in their proposal.

Although there was a growing consensus to amend the Transportation Act, many carriers and business groups opposed it. Baltimore and Ohio Railroad President Daniel Willard wrote President Coolidge that no one was completely happy with the legislation, but that amending it should wait until it was clear exactly how it should be altered.[14] Willard, as he often did, took a more moderate view. Others no doubt agreed with Atterbury, who told an Ohio audience that the carriers should be completely free of all government regulation.[15]

The Legislative Battle: Round One

The unions asked Senator Howell and Representative Barkley—both members of the Interstate and Foreign Commerce Committees in their respective houses—to introduce their proposal, which they did on February 28, 1924. Passage of the bill seemed unlikely because of its pro-labor nature; still the unions mobilized their membership to write their congressmen and senators asking for their support.[16] The letter-writing campaign failed, but it helped to make revision of the Transportation Act an important election-year issue.

Although President Coolidge favored changing labor policy, he did not take an active role in revising it; he urged the parties to negotiate an accept-able compromise. The carriers remained staunchly opposed to revision and asked their supporters to write their legislators voicing their dissent. The opposition's criticisms generally revolved around two principal arguments. One was that the Howell-Barkley Bill did not protect the public interest be-cause disputes were to be solved by representatives chosen by the unions and the carriers. Lack of public representation would be a long step backwards, Alfred Thom, general counsel of the Association of Railroad Executives, informed President Coolidge.[17] The second argument was that if Congress abolished the RLB, wages would rise, causing rates to increase. Because they would be forced to join one of the standard organizations, company unions and unorganized workers opposed the legislation, giving the carriers' com-plaints legitimacy.[18]

Strong carrier opposition doomed the Howell-Barkley Bill. Carriers and their allies were simply not going to allow a bill to pass that they viewed as pro-labor. The initial Senate committee hearings were held on March 18, and labor presented its arguments. The carriers asked for more time to prepare their rebuttal and were granted ten days. Labor's chances were also hindered because Senator La Follette was too ill to attend. The bill languished while he recuperated. Within hours of his return, he forced the committee to vote, and it passed, 10–3.[19]

In the House, the debate on the bill led to a bitter but important confron-tation. Samuel E. Winslow (R-MA), who chaired the Committee on Foreign and Interstate Commerce, and House Speaker Nicholas Longworth (R-OH) opposed the bill. Winslow refused to allow it to be voted on; he claimed that hearings would be too expensive, and since the measure was unlikely to pass, debate was useless. Proponents had one option. Under House rules a bill could be removed from committee and brought to the floor if 150 mem-bers signed a discharge petition.[20] Barkley eventually gathered the necessary signatures, invoking the rule for the first time. The House voted, 194–181, to release the bill.[21]

Barkley made a motion to begin debate on the bill, but the presiding offi-cer ruled it out of order. Opponents, led by Everett Sanders (R-IN) and Long-worth, contended that because the bill contained an appropriations clause, it never fell under the jurisdiction of the Commerce Committee and, therefore, was not properly on the calendar.[22] The renewed opposition and the ruling not to debate the Howell-Barkley Bill ended any chance that it would move forward in the current congressional session, which ended in June.[23] Unionists were perhaps disappointed, but not surprised. They expected strong opposition in the House, and correctly assumed that their supporters would be able to get the bill out of committee to the floor.[24] The assertion that the bill should not have been submitted to the Commerce Committee was not anticipated. Opponents challenged the bill based on a technicality rather than its content.

The defeat gave labor an important political asset: the petition to release the bill from the Commerce Committee. In the 1920 campaign, the unions used the roll call vote on the Esch-Cummins Bill as an effective tool, and intended to use the same tactic in 1924, using the release petition as their litmus test. One member who felt the wrath of the workers was BLE member Representative John Cooper (R-OH). He opposed the Howell-Barkley Bill. Readers of the *Firemen's Magazine* were told, "He is unworthy of the vote of a single wage earner and a special effort should be put forth to acquaint every man and woman working for wages in his district of his anti-labor attitude."[25] Cooper managed to keep his seat for more than a decade, losing his bid for reelection in 1936.

Railroad labor was optimistic about its political future in early 1924, not only because the Railway Labor Bill was about to be introduced. In a special election the previous summer, Magnus Johnson, Farmer-Labor, won a seat in the U.S. Senate from Minnesota, which not only gave labor one more friend in the Senate, but also cut the GOP's majority.[26] The labor press noted with enthusiasm the victories of Labor parties in Europe, especially Great Britain in January. The *Firemen's Magazine* wrote that Ramsey MacDonald's victory " . . . is surely the subject of felicitation and congratulation for the labor movement of every other country."[27] Buoyed by their success in the 1922 elections, the victory of Johnson, and labor victories in Europe, the railroad brotherhoods and their partners approached the 1924 elections with optimism. One other sign—albeit symbolic—of labor's changing attitude toward politics occurred when the BLE amended its constitution to allow it to become more active politically through greater education and use of the ballot box. Only a decade earlier the union had banned political discussion on the job.[28]

Congress adjourned in June without acting on the Howell-Barkley Bill, but labor was not discouraged and, along with the rest of the nation, turned its attention to the upcoming political conventions. Meeting in Cleveland, in what the *Firemen's Magazine* called the largest gathering of political reactionaries since the Chamber of Commerce convention, Republicans nominated Calvin Coolidge, who had been president since the previous August when Warren Harding died. According to the labor press, the only progressive thing about the convention was its use of the radio.[29] Only La Follette offered opposition, albeit weak, to Silent Cal. The only suspense involved who would be the vice presidential nominee. Ultimately, Charles Dawes, an Illinois banker known for his anti-labor position, received the nod.

Democrats and progressives hoped to capitalize on Teapot Dome and the other Harding-era scandals. The scandals, however, proved more destructive to the Democrats, especially to William McAdoo, one of the party's frontrunners. He campaigned vigorously in the early primaries, winning against a number of minor, usually favorite son, candidates. The lengthening shadow of Teapot Dome, however, engulfed McAdoo. Oil magnate Edward L. Doheny, whose name became synonymous with the scandal, was a leading California Democrat. Earlier he had hired McAdoo's Los Angeles law firm on a $50,000 annual retainer. Doheny also employed as legal counsel three other members of Wilson's cabinet: Thomas W. Gregory, Lindley Garrison, and Franklin K. Lane. There was no evidence of illegality in these relationships. However, the mere suggestion of impropriety destroyed McAdoo's presidential hopes.[30] He considered withdrawing, but after consulting with allies, decided to continue. He was clearly the frontrunner and considered by many to be Wilson's heir apparent.[31]

Several factors prompted New York Governor Alfred E. Smith to enter the Democratic race. As governor of the nation's largest state and having easily won reelection by a plurality of nearly four hundred thousand votes, he was automatically a presidential contender if he chose to enter the race. He was especially concerned by McAdoo's association with Doheny and his financial backing from millionaires Thomas Chadbourne and Barnard Baruch. New York Democrats were anxious to have Smith run, and he was clearly flattered by their enthusiasm when, on April 15, the state party convention passed a resolution supporting his nomination. The New Yorkers' symbolic resolution was the culmination of a steady movement on the part of Smith toward running.[32]

Governor Smith's decision to enter the race further divided the already sharply split party. Two factions formed as the convention convened at Madison Square Garden in late June. Smith's supporters tended to be urban, Roman Catholic, immigrants or their children, wet, and sensitive to the Teapot Dome scandal. McAdoo's partisans were more likely to be rural, Protestant, dry, and not particularly concerned with the scandal. The two most significant cleavages were between urban Roman Catholics and rural Protestants, and the other—arguably most divisive—issue was the Ku Klux Klan, which supported McAdoo. Although McAdoo, a native of Tennessee, favored a plank supporting racial tolerance, he did not, nor had he ever, specifically renounced the KKK. The fight over the racial plank was an indication of the sharp divisions within the party. Amidst chaos and under the watchful eyes of a thousand newly arrived New York police officers, the convention narrowly failed to condemn the Ku Klux Klan by name.[33]

Not surprisingly, the Democrats were too sharply divided to agree on a candidate. The raucous Tammany Hall partisans of Smith who dominated the galleries of Madison Square Garden only made matters worse. At one point, future president and nominal head of Smith's campaign, Franklin D. Roosevelt, sent a note up to the balcony demanding that the person responsible for a loud siren stop using it.[34] After nearly two weeks, on the 103rd ballot, John W. Davis, a Wall Street attorney, won the nomination. While the convention will always be remembered for its length and for the floor battle, it was also the last convention for William Jennings Bryan, who was in the thick of the battle over the Ku Klux Klan. He died the following summer. The convention also marked the return of Franklin D. Roosevelt, who nominated Smith with an impassioned speech that sent Smith loyalists into frenzied demonstrations of support for the "Happy Warrior."[35]

As the Democratic convention approached, many people hoped that the party would nominate a progressive candidate. Davis was not acceptable to railroad labor, which had remained loyal to McAdoo. Telegrams from railroad men poured in to him. "Dear Bill," one telegram began, "Pardon me for calling you Bill but that is all railroad men know you by is our big Bill."[36] Keating, editor of *Labor* and a former Democratic congressman, perhaps summed up the feelings of many Democrats when years later he wrote that neither Smith nor McAdoo gave a hoot for the party.[37]

Like the nominating process, the platform reflected deep schisms within the party. Historian David Burner wrote, " . . . its sympathies were as wide as its recommendations thin."[38] Concerning railroad labor, the platform conceded that the Transportation Act was a failure and vaguely called for revision that would be in the interest of " . . . public welfare."[39]

The nomination of Davis and the profound divisions within the party were clear indications of the troubled state of the Democrats in 1924 and opened the door for a third-party candidate. Since 1920, La Follette and other progressives had let it be known that if the two parties chose "reactionaries" in 1924, they might launch a Progressive Party or at least a presidential candidate. As early as the autumn of 1922 the senator's advisors outlined their plans for an independent presidential campaign.[40]

Delegates to the CPPA convention who met in Cleveland in the summer of 1924 faced a crucial question: should they endorse a third-party candidate or should they take a bolder step and form a third party? The Socialists wanted to form a third party, but the La Follette camp and the RLEA opposed the idea. To avoid a potentially embarrassing bit of political drama—that is, having to accept or decline the nomination of a Progressive Party—La Follette and his allies arranged for him to accept the endorsement of the convention while remaining an independent candidate and not a nominee of the Progressive Party. The La Follette for President Committee presented him with a petition signed by two hundred thousand people asking him to run, which convinced him, so he announced his candidacy on July 3, the day before the convention officially began.[41]

With La Follette's candidacy endorsed and the question of the third party delayed, the convention turned its attention to the platform, which concisely articulated many issues that progressives had cared about for a generation or more. Most importantly for the railway operatives, it called for repeal of the Transportation Act; immediate passage of the Howell-Barkley Bill; and for rail rates to be based upon actual, prudent investment and cost of service. La Follette's platform and the CPPA's, which were technically separate documents, declared that public ownership of the railroads was the ultimate solution to problems in the industry.[42] There is little evidence that the brotherhoods or other railroad unions still seriously considered government ownership of the carriers a solution.

The threat of a third party, however, influenced the thinking of the Republicans in 1924. Although the majority of union leaders never seriously considered forming a third party, their posturing and leadership in the CPPA posed a potential threat to the two parties.[43] Ben E. Chapin, editor of the *Railroad Employee,* advised one of President Coolidge's personal secretaries that President Stone of the BLE was " . . . exerting every possible effort to bring about the organization of a third party."[44] Chapin's statement

Figure 6. John M. Baer (R-ND) frequently drew cartoons for *Labor*. He served in the House from 1917 to 1920. This cartoon celebrated the power of independent, nonpartisan voters in the days before the election.

was inaccurate, but a third party posed a risk that the White House did not take lightly. Republican policy makers could not be assured of La Follette's position prior to the convention. It is unlikely that La Follette thought he could win the election, but according to *Labor's* editor, Keating, the senator hoped that he could injure President Coolidge the same way that Theodore Roosevelt damaged President Taft in 1912. By gaining the balance of power in the Electoral College, the senator hoped to lay the foundation for a Progressive Party.[45]

The GOP was more aggressive than the Democrats in courting labor's vote in 1924. Republican hostility toward labor reached its apex in the fall of 1922 when Attorney General Daugherty summarily ended the shopmen's strike by convincing a judge to issue the infamous injunction. By the summer of 1924, the party's attitude had shifted. The GOP platform reflected the growing concern over labor relations and the threat of a third party headed by the railroad brotherhoods. Its railroad plank supported revision of Title III to meet " . . . the requirements made evident by experience gained from its actual creation." Written by Senator Albert Cummins of Iowa, it endorsed collective bargaining, voluntary mediation, and arbitration as the most important steps in maintaining peaceful labor relations. It also proposed the creation of an impartial emergency tribunal to investigate the conflicts and publish its conclusions. Addressing labor in general, the Republicans urged state legislatures to consider the child labor amendment, and took credit for abolition of the twelve-hour day and seven-day work week.[46] The GOP platform language concerning railroad labor was similar to the Howell-Barkley Bill, but was sufficiently vague so as not to upset more business-oriented constituents, especially the carriers.

The Democratic platform was more ambiguous. While it endorsed the goals of the Transportation Act, it conceded that the act failed to meet expectations, but offered no clear-cut solution. It endorsed collective bargaining but proposed no legislative action.[47] Clearly neither the Democrats nor the Republicans were aggressively courting the railroaders' votes, but both recognized that workers could not be ignored. It is therefore evident that the threat of a third party influenced the two major parties.

Both President Coolidge and Davis made it clear that they wanted to garner workers' support by addressing their concerns at Labor Day rallies. While La Follette's first campaign speech fell back on progressive rhetoric by attacking monopolies, Davis took a more aggressive stance than his party's platform by endorsing the child labor law and revision of Title III.[48] President Coolidge restated his support for the party's planks concerning railroad labor and the RLB. He also discussed the advances in wages and reduction in hours that most American workers had enjoyed since the end of World War I. Referring to these gains he said, "This has been brought about by the general recognition that on the whole labor leaders are square, and on the whole employers intend to be fair." He called the RLB an interesting experiment in railroad labor relations and suggested that, "It could probably be modified, through mutual agreement, to the benefit of all concerned."[49]

Daniel Willard, president of the Baltimore and Ohio Railroad, agreed with the president and warned him that most people in the railroad industry had " . . . lost confidence in the agencies created by the Transportation Act." Willard echoed the president's notion that railroad management and union leaders should meet. Coolidge requested that Willard keep him informed of the situation and that he write him again after the election.[50]

The Election

With enthusiasm for La Follette running high immediately after the Cleveland convention, he set about trying to establish a campaign organization. Because he refused to run on a party ticket, it was exceedingly difficult for his supporters to organize themselves into an effective campaign organization. Eventually the various groups selected Wisconsin Congressman John M. Nelson as campaign chairman and Robert La Follette Jr. as vice chairman. The campaign structure was never really satisfactory, and there was constant bickering, but the senator remained aloof, preserving his strength for a series of campaign speeches.[51]

From the beginning, La Follette faced an uphill battle. He was never able to overcome the twin obstacles that independent candidates often face: lack of money and a national organization. Arguably, the most debilitating problem remained insufficient funding. La Follette's supporters hoped to raise $3 million, but collected only $460,000. Some of the money came from the sale of campaign paraphernalia, and funds were so short that officials occasionally charged admission to campaign speeches or passed the hat. Often requests for literature and other material were only partially filled or not met at all.[52] La Follette also had to contend with the possibility that his political enemies would intercept campaign literature. For that reason L. J. Niemchesky, La Follette's director of distribution, warned a campaign worker to make sure there was nothing on the outside of the package to indicate it was from La Follette's headquarters.[53] Progressives also found it impossible to overcome the handicap of not having a national organization. The CPPA had organizations in thirty states and union efforts helped, but La Follette still had difficulties getting on the ballot in some states.

The GOP platform made continuing support of La Follette politically risky for the railroad unions. Perhaps the clearest indication of the unions' tepid support of La Follette was their stinginess. The brotherhoods and the AFL, with combined membership of approximately three million, contributed a paltry $75,000.[54] With passage of the Howell-Barkley Bill or, as was more likely, similar legislation on the horizon, vigorous support of La Follette could prove to be a huge political mistake for the brotherhoods.

In congressional races the unions used the same nonpartisan approach that they had in 1922. The RLEA appointed a committee headed by Bert M. Jewell of the RED to examine the records of all candidates. The labor press urged the rank-and-file to vote for progressive candidates because La Follette, workers were warned, would be crippled by a hostile Congress. Labor publications printed a list of candidates that members should support. Some unions sent letters directly to their membership suggesting who deserved their vote. One such letter, sent to the membership of the United Brotherhood of Maintenance of Way Employees in Massachusetts, said the incumbent Senator David I. Walsh, " . . . has practically a 100% record and should by all means be re-elected." The letter then chronicled his voting record. Conversely, the letter said of Samuel E. Winslow, their recent adversary when the Howell-Barkley Bill was being considered, he " . . . is not seeking re-election. However, if he were, his record would require that he be opposed and defeated." Labor scored important victories in the primaries, including the defeat of six of the most objectionable, reactionary senators.[55]

The results of the November elections were not as favorable as labor had hoped.[56] President Coolidge won with 15.7 million votes, outpolling the combined total of Davis (8.3 million) and La Follette (4.8 million). Many of the nation's farmers became suddenly less progressive when wheat prices rose in the fall, generally bringing them to their highest levels in nearly four years. Analysis of La Follette's vote total reveals the regional nature of his support. He won only Wisconsin, and finished second in North Dakota, Montana, Wyoming, Idaho, Nevada, Washington, and California. Of the 236 counties that he won, only two outside of Wisconsin were east of the Mississippi River—Clinton in Illinois and Dade in Florida.[57]

Although La Follette's showing was disappointing, progressives remained optimistic; the CPPA helped to elect fourteen senators.[58] The Republicans had a majority of fifteen in the Senate, but five senators were considered La Follette progressives so the party leadership could not count on their loyalty. Progressives claimed that a similar situation could be found in the House of Representatives. Many progressives, including La Follette, believed that the election results indicated the beginning of a significant realignment of the American political landscape.[59] La Follette's death seven month later effectively ended any serious attempt by progressives to form a third party. Despite the funding woes and lack of a sufficient organization, the only third-party candidates to gain a greater percentage of the popular vote were Theodore Roosevelt in 1912 and H. Ross Perot in 1992. Clearly, La Follette struck a chord with many who believed that neither the Democrats nor the Republicans addressed their concerns.

Conclusion

The elections of 1924 thus brought the first stage of railroad labor's battle to abolish the Railroad Labor Board to a close. Since the midterm election of 1922, the railroad unions had remained politically viable, expanding their political activities—if not their power—in the lean years. The RLEA and the CPPA, formed in 1922, were instrumental in promoting labor's agenda. The unions presented the Howell-Barkley Bill to Congress and forced the GOP to recognize the need to amend the Transportation Act. Although the progressive vote was not enough in the minds of railroad union leaders to warrant the formation of a third party, it was clear that the RLB had lost the favor of the administration and that a new approach had to found.

A writer for *Railway Age* declared after the election that the victory of Coolidge and the Republicans " . . . seems to place the country squarely behind the transportation plank of the Republican platform . . . favoring 'a stable, consistent and constructive policy towards the railroads.'"[60] Union leaders continued to work behind the scenes to strengthen their position. By remaining politically active, and even threatening to some, the brotherhoods assured themselves a voice in the creation of the new legislation.

· 6 ·

The Railway Labor Act

The second stage of labor's campaign to repeal Title III of the Transportation Act, which created the RLB, began in the autumn of 1924. Although the union-sponsored Howell-Barkley Bill did not become law in the spring, the unions remained optimistic. The election of 1924 offered unions another opportunity to promote labor reform and it marked the beginning of their final push to enact satisfactory reform legislation. The Railway Labor Act, signed into law in May 1926, was the culmination of labor's four-year battle to abolish the RLB; it also ushered in a new era in labor relations. Railroad labor, management, and the federal government established a new cooperative relationship and accompanying institutions that served as models for the future.[1]

Even as the election approached, the brotherhoods prepared for the next round of their fight to abolish the RLB.[2] In early October David B. Robertson, president of the BLFE, and L. G. Griffing, president of the BLE, requested, and were granted, a meeting with President Coolidge.[3] It is impossible to know exactly what transpired at the meeting. It is unlikely that the men discussed the World Series, won by the hometown Washington Senators; a more likely topic of conversation was the upcoming election. Given labor's reluctance to donate badly needed money to Robert La Follette's campaign and its immediate abandonment of the progressive coalition after the election, it seems likely that the union leaders struck a deal, or perhaps it would be better to say reached an understanding, with President Coolidge. To reach any accord with the labor representatives, Mr. Coolidge would have had to agree to support some sort of railroad labor reform. Given the GOP's labor plank and his previous statements, it seems likely that the president would have been willing to accommodate the union leaders. In principle, all agreed that the railroad industry needed some kind of labor reform.

Later in October Stone called a meeting of the RLEA to convene after the election on November 8. The principal topics on the agenda were developing a strategy for the upcoming fight in Congress over the Howell-Barkley Bill, and clarifying their position on a third party.[4] No doubt the results of the meeting with Coolidge were also discussed.

The union leaders were pragmatic. On November 8 the RLEA voted to abandon La Follette's fledgling coalition. They feared that any action that could be interpreted as radical would be counterproductive to their ultimate goal: abolishing the RLB. They would not do anything to undermine their political influence.[5] A delegation of labor leaders went to La Follette's home outside of Madison to deliver the bad news. The disappointed senator told the committee that he would take their news under " . . . prayerful consideration." He wanted to continue the fight.

The withdrawal of the rail unions from the coalition made it very unlikely that a third party would be created.[6] All possibility ended when Senator La Follette died in June 1925. Progressives briefly courted Nebraska's GOP Senator George Norris, but he was not enthusiastic. No one assumed La Follette's mantle of leadership. With his death so too died any chance of a Progressive Party emerging out of the dying embers of the nation's progressive movement. Progressive groups that favored a third party withdrew from the CPPA and tried to establish a party early in 1925, but ultimately failed. The CPPA remained but had little significance. Although the railroad unions dominated CPPA, they preferred to work through the RLEA.[7]

With their position concerning La Follette and a third party clear, the unions focused their attention exclusively on destroying the RLB. When Congress reconvened in December the unions had two reasons for optimism. First, Barkley had maneuvered the bill to a preferred position on the House calendar, which meant it would be considered on the first and third Monday of each month until definite action was taken. Secondly, Sen. Cummins had become an unlikely ally. His authorship of the Transportation Act had won him the enmity of railroad unions. However, Cummins was not vehemently anti-union or indifferent to union political power. He had lost his chairmanship of the Senate Interstate and Foreign Commerce Committee when progressive Republicans on the committee voted for Democrat Ellison Smith of Georgia.[8]

It is difficult to discern Cummins' motivation. In his mid-seventies, perhaps he did not want his legacy to be the Transportation Act, which most people acknowledged needed revision. He wrote the Republican labor plank of the party's 1924 platform and after the election began working with the unions to reach a compromise on the legislation. Like many observers who were concerned with the railroad labor question, Cummins favored continuation of the RLB, but understood the potentially serious consequences of strife in the railroad industry. Publicly he stated that he believed that with revisions the Howell-Barkley Bill might be acceptable. On November 25 he met with Jewell for three and a half hours. After the meeting Jewell said Cummins " . . . seemingly was very desirous of being of assistance in passage of the bill."[9]

The unions' efforts received a further boost when President Coolidge, in his message to Congress on December 3, called for revision of the labor section of the Transportation Act. He reiterated some of his party's campaign rhetoric. In cautious language he supported the principles of collective bargaining and conciliation, mediation, and voluntary arbitration, but he did not endorse the Howell-Barkley Bill by name.[10] Seemingly, Coolidge's only reservation was that he wanted a provision, as stated in the GOP platform, which created an Emergency Board. Proponents of the measure, including Cummins and Barkley, thought his message was a ringing endorsement of the bill. Coolidge, however, told Cummins that he did not intend to back the Howell-Barkley Bill. The president later clarified his position, saying he hoped satisfactory machinery would be established.[11]

As the unions pursued a political and legislative solution to the RLB problem, matters concerning railroad labor continued to wind their way through the courts. The U.S. Supreme Court issued a ruling that further upset the delicate balance. The case before the Supreme Court, *Pennsylvania Railroad v. The United States Railroad Labor Board*, began when the RLB issued Decision 119 on April 14, 1921, which stated that the national agreements governing working rules and conditions would be terminated on July 1, 1921. Further, it stated that new agreements were to be negotiated separately by each carrier and its employees or lawful organizations, agreed to by a majority of a particular class of employees. The RLB decision stated that representatives chosen by workers, "whether employees of a particular carrier or otherwise, shall be agreed to by management."[12]

This decision seemed to lay a solid foundation for unions to represent workers, and, of course, would mean that wartime organizational gains were less jeopardized. Writing for the majority, Chief Justice William Howard Taft argued that it was clearly congressional intent, and in the highest public interest, to prevent the interruption of commerce. The ruling, however, did anything but promote a climate where commerce would be uninterrupted. The Supreme Court also ruled that Congress had not granted the RLB power to enforce its decisions, except through moral sanction of public opinion, and did not grant rights enforceable in a court of law.[13]

The ruling severely damaged the board's power and credibility. It increased the possibility of renewed labor strife by opening the door more widely for company unions. Carriers, such as the Pennsylvania, routinely consented to bargain only with workers who represented company-sponsored unions or associations. Given time, those carriers that dealt in good faith with unions may have refused to deal with those unions as well. Most observers recognized that some regulation was needed in the industry. It was against this backdrop of assault, not only on railroad labor, but also on all labor through the pernicious American Plan, that the shopmen's strike occurred in 1922.

Publicly the carriers remained opposed to revision of the Transportation Act, but they also realized that the court's ruling might create severe labor problems. Privately they moved toward cooperation, but were rebuffed. They advocated repeal of Title III, reinstating mediation machinery first established in the Newlands Act and extending its scope to include all employees, and the creation of an Emergency Board. The unions, however, refused to support any new initiatives so long as the Howell-Barkley Bill remained on the table.[14]

While the unions refused to discuss the carriers' proposal, they also retreated from pushing the bill on the Hill. Instead they tried to cooperate more closely with the administration, assuming that the best chance for victory lay in the White House. Between the end of November and January, Secretary of Commerce Herbert Hoover and Cummins, acting as representatives for the administration, held several conferences with union leaders to discuss the situation.[15]

Once rebuffed, the carriers ignored mounting pressure to negotiate a settlement, refusing to cooperate ostensibly because Jewell, who was a key figure in the shopmen's strike of 1922, was on the unions' negotiating committee. Jewell stepped aside, but the carriers continued to delay. At its annual meeting in November, the ARE held that railroad problems should be dealt with as economic issues, not political concerns. The ARE argued that if weaknesses in the Transportation Act became apparent, they should be handled " . . . after a fair and judicial consideration of all pertinent economic facts, and not as the result of political agitation or of political pressure on Congress."[16] Even the usually conservative industry journal *Railway Age* argued that experimentation in labor relations might be needed. The journal ventured that a policy that broke away from both autocratic management and unionism would be appropriate.[17]

Because labor sought to gain the administration's cooperation and to demonstrate its goodwill to the carriers, the unions asked Barkley not to bring the bill to the floor of the House during its second session. The RLEA decided, however, to renew its efforts in the Senate. They did so only after Daniel Willard of the Baltimore and Ohio said he would meet with a delegation, but then refused to return phone calls. No one thought the bill had much chance of being passed, but unionists and their allies hoped the public debate would prod the carriers into cooperation, which it did not. Still, labor leaders believed that as a result of their efforts most members of Congress understood the RLB's "uselessness and menacing qualities."[18]

Although labor was making progress, it was growing impatient with the carriers and with newspaper reports. Union leaders believed that the carriers were encouraging stories that misrepresented their position. In February the RLEA asserted: "They [the carriers] are not working to preserve peace. They are fomenting war." Further, they called the carriers' activities "provocative" and asserted that their actions could lead to strikes. The carriers' most potent argument against revision was that the public would not be represented in dispute settlements under the provisions of the proposed bill. The unions took issue with the carriers' assessment. Donald Richberg, the unions' legal counsel, claimed that 185 of the nation's 200 leading newspapers reported erroneously that the public would be eliminated from the settlement process. He pointed out that the Howell-Barkley Bill called for a five-member board, appointed by the president, to settle disputes that could not be resolved through conferences. He charged that the carriers exploited "popular ignorance" and reported that the proposed Boards of Adjustment would be substitutes for the RLB. Richberg said that this was a misrepresentation reported by the Associated Press.[19]

The unwillingness of the carriers to bargain, except on their own terms, stalled the negotiations. The ARE wanted to maintain the status quo; it continued to argue that the Transportation Act should be allowed to function under normal business conditions, which it insisted had not existed consistently since the law's enactment. By doing this, the ARE argued that more precise amendments could be written.[20] On March 10, 1925, Robertson met with Secretary of Labor James Davis, who had replaced Hoover as the administration's chief negotiator. Robertson reported back to his colleagues that Davis seemed to agree that revision of Title III was necessary and that, if the carriers would not bargain, they should accept the administration's proposal.[21]

Compliance

Just when it appeared that overtures to convince the carriers to negotiate had failed, two developments occurred that reinvigorated the bargaining process. The United States Supreme Court handed down a second crucial decision in the *Pennsylvania Railroad System and Allied Lines Federation No. 90 v. the Pennsylvania Railroad Company, et al.*, which restored some of the RLB's lost prestige. Labor leaders hoped that the court's decision would oblige the carriers to return to the bargaining table and convince Congress of the need to pass the legislation.[22] A second decisive event involved the engineers and firemen, whose leaders refused to appear before the RLB even after being subpoenaed by a federal judge.

The second Supreme Court decision grew out of the same conflict between the Pennsylvania and its employees that it had ruled on in 1921. After the first decision the carrier still refused to negotiate new working rules with delegates elected by System Federation No. 90. The union and the company held separate elections as directed by the RLB. The railroad refused to recognize the men elected by the System Federation, declaring that it would deal only with representatives chosen in the company-sponsored elections. The union sued for monetary damages because the company enacted changes in rules based upon agreements reached with workers not recognized by the union.

The primary issue before the court was congressional intent. The court ruled that by ignoring the RLB decision, which ordered the Pennsylvania to negotiate with duly elected union representatives, the carrier violated congressional intent, which was that labor and management bargain in good faith. The carrier would only recognize representatives elected by the company union, which did not represent a majority of workers. Chief Justice William

Howard Taft, writing for the majority, stated that the Pennsylvania Railroad Company used every endeavor to avoid compliance with the judgment and principles of the RLB. The ruling stopped short of making company unions illegal, but it put their existence on tenuous footing if they did not represent a majority of workers. It also made it clear that defying an RLB ruling would be interpreted as an attempt to circumvent the intent of the law, which, according to the court, was to ensure the efficient operation of the nation's railroads. The Transportation Act provided no enforcement mechanism except public opinion and did not make compliance with RLB rulings compulsory. Thus politicians feared that the second decision would lead to destructive industrial conflict.[23] While the ruling may have enhanced the RLB's prestige, it did not give it specific enforcement power. Even had the ruling given more robust power to the RLB, it is doubtful the unions would have responded positively because the board was so thoroughly discredited in their estimation.

The second event that prompted the carriers into action was a wage dispute that involved the engineers and firemen. The feud between the unions and southwestern carriers, led by the Southern Pacific, began in October 1923 when the unions began negotiating with the carriers nationally for a 5 percent wage increase with no significant changes in work rules. The New York Central granted the unions' request in January 1924, and most carriers quickly followed suit, except in the southwest where negotiations continued. Soon talks broke down, forcing labor to deal with each carrier separately. Although neither party requested the RLB's assistance, it interceded when negotiations failed. The board ordered a hearing, but union officials refused to participate, arguing that the RLB acted unlawfully by intervening when the case had not been officially submitted. At the request of the board, Federal Judge James Wilkerson issued a subpoena compelling BLFE president Robertson and John McGuire of the BLE to appear before the board. Both men refused, and the case went to the Supreme Court.[24]

While the parties waited for the court's decision, the unions issued a strike ballot. As the engineers and firemen voted, the RLB granted the 5 percent wage increase, but also made significant changes in work rules that practically nullified the raise. The unions asserted that they would ignore the RLB, and the carriers agreed to reopen negotiations, avoiding a potentially damaging strike. The parties reached an agreement, and the rest of the roads in the region quickly followed suit.

In the wage controversy the unions took bold, decisive steps. Almost a year later, as Congress neared the conclusion of its debate on the Railway Labor Bill, *Railway Age* stated that the principal development that changed the attitude of the carriers was the success of the engineers and firemen when they threatened to strike and disobeyed the subpoenas.[25] Clearly, by the spring of 1925, the unions—or at least the leadership—were increasingly frustrated and angry over the carriers' behavior concerning RLB rulings.

In March 1925, as the wage controversy neared its conclusion and shortly after the second Supreme Court ruling, the carriers finally took steps to begin bargaining with the unions. Just two weeks after the court's second Pennsylvania decision, the ARE appointed a subcommittee to begin discussions with the RLEA concerning revision of Title III. Now the unions dragged their feet; they did not appoint a committee until July because Congress was not in session.[26]

After several preliminary meetings between Robertson and W. W. Atterbury of the Pennsylvania line, who represented the carriers, the full committees met in New York City on August 13.[27] The meeting lasted only ninety minutes, but the groups agreed that they were not far apart on several key points: that joint conferences between unions and carriers should be the essential component of solving disputes; that mediation and voluntary arbitration should follow if conciliation failed; that some form of Adjustment Boards should be created; and that the law should grant the president authority to appoint a fact-finding commission to investigate unsolved disputes if they threatened to create a national crisis. Each side appointed two men to complete the negotiations.[28]

The four men went to work immediately, using the Howell-Barkley Bill as the basis for their negotiation.[29] The negotiations were carried out in secret, partly because the union leaders did not want the rank and file to know about the meetings. The new bill would not be as favorable to unions as the Howell-Barkley Bill, and the labor organizations were forced to make difficult compromises. At the first meeting the carriers objected to the inclusion of subordinate officials in the bargaining units. "Subordinate official" was a nebulous job classification that referred to men in low-level management positions, some of whom were union members who had been promoted to white-collar jobs. The carriers also wanted to eliminate the proposed penalty for changing work rules and wages without warning and opposed any provisions compelling the creation of National Boards of Adjustment or an

Emergency Board. The original bill contained strong language to prevent the formation of company unions. The carriers naturally objected and wanted that language softened.[30] Labor, of course, objected to the carriers' suggestions. The committee charged Elisha Lee of the Pennsylvania with the difficult task of reconciling the two proposals.

The subcommittees met again in mid-September to review the proposal. The carriers made several concessions. They fully approved the provisions of the Howell-Barkley Bill on filing awards with the appropriate district court, which would give the rulings legal authority. Robertson reported to his colleagues that the carriers accepted the original bill's provisions regarding mediation "almost as whole." The new proposal called for a Board of Mediation and Conciliation patterned after the boards created under the Erdman Act of 1898 and the Newlands Act of 1913; it would be a five-member body appointed by the president. None of the members were to be associated with labor or management. The board's functions were threefold: to induce the parties to settle disputes that could not be settled in conference or before the proper Board of Adjustment; to settle disagreements concerning wages and work rules when conferences could not reach an agreement; and to convince the parties to submit their differences to arbitration and to help organize arbitration proceedings.[31]

The most significant difference that remained concerned the Boards of Adjustment. The original union proposal called for compulsory local and national boards. The new plan called for the voluntary creation of the boards. If they were not created, the disputes would be referred to the Board of Mediation, which was to have the power to convene a Board of Adjustment if it could not settle the dispute. To the unions, the subcommittee's proposal was unacceptable. Labor considered the National Boards of Adjustment the cardinal virtue of the United States Railroad Administration and the centerpiece of the Howell-Barkley Bill. The Transportation Act made the Boards of Adjustment voluntary, and thus very few were created. As a result, the RLB received far more cases than anticipated. The ARE did not approve of the new draft; it argued that the Board of Mediation should solve a dispute if no Board of Adjustment had been created.[32]

Previous railroad labor bills generally only covered the operating employees, but the proposal broke important new ground. The final version of the Railway Labor Act defined subordinate officials and railroad employees as " . . . every person in the service of the carrier, subject to its continuing authority . . . who performs any work defined as that of employes [*sic*] or subordinate officials."[33]

Ultimately, the carriers prevailed on many key issues. Labor lost the argument for mandatory Boards of Adjustment. The final bill stated: "Boards of Adjustment shall be created by agreement between any carrier or group of carriers, or carriers as a whole, and its or their employees." Many within the labor camp did not approve of this critical concession.[34] The unions also made a significant concession on the issue of company unions. Richberg's associate, David Lilienthal, who did much of the research and writing of the Howell-Barkley Bill, thought the bill "sounds the knell of Atterburyism" because any effort to influence or participate in the choice of labor's conferees was illegal. The RLA, however, allowed a carrier and its employees to settle disputes through mutually established machinery.[35]

The unions made two other concessions. Section 6 of the Howell-Barkley Bill set current wages as the permanent minimum, to prevent reductions such as those ordered by the RLB, which had triggered the shopmen's strike, but that provision was not included in the Railway Labor Act.[36] The unions also agreed to forfeit their right to strike from the time the president created the Emergency Board until thirty days after it issued its report. The carriers, too, were bound not to change working conditions, which could be altered by agreement only.[37] This concession limited the effective use of the strike as a weapon in labor's arsenal.

In late December the ARE requested one more conference with the unions. President Coolidge, in his December 8, 1925, message to Congress, announced that an accord was nearly complete and that, as long as both sides agreed and the public remained protected, he would sign it.[38] On January 4 the draft bill was sent to the labor executives, and two days later both the carriers and labor approved it.[39] The following day the labor leaders met with President Coolidge and informed him that the proposal was ready to be introduced. The chairmen of the Interstate and Foreign Commerce Committees, Representative James Parker (R-NY), and Senator James Watson (R-IN), introduced the bill on January 8, 1926, and within a week the Senate committee began hearings on the Watson-Parker Bill. The spirit of cooperation that marked the bargaining process also permeated the hearings as the bill moved quickly through both houses.

Robertson mobilized the RLEA members; he asked that each union send at least one lobbyist to Washington.[40] There was only minor opposition to the bill, which came mostly from groups such as the National Association of Manufacturers, the National Grange, and the American Farm Bureau. Carriers representing about 15 percent of the nation's rail miles also opposed the bill.[41]

For the most part Congress turned a deaf ear to the complaints of opponents. There was one serious attempt to amend the legislation when Representative Homer Hoch (R-KS) offered an amendment that would have given more power to the Interstate Commerce Commission (ICC). He posed an argument based on protecting consumers' rights and low prices. The ICC would have little choice but to raise freight and passenger rates when the Board of Mediation handed down arbitration awards. The amendment, which opponents defeated, would have permitted the ICC to consider the "merits of any such arbitration award when determining freight or passenger rates or other changes."[42] The only amendment that passed clarified the definition of carriers so that street, suburban, and interurban carriers would be excluded. The bill passed the House on March 1 by a 381–13 vote.[43]

Opponents in the Senate attacked the bill with much vigor, but could not attach any amendments. Richberg, Alfred Thom, the ARE's general counsel, and Atterbury all spoke against the proposed changes. Senators Norris and Robert La Follette Jr. (R-WI) organized proponents to defeat any proposed changes. The Senate approved it in the same form as the House, and the president signed it into law on May 20, 1926.[44] (Senator La Follette won a special election shortly after his father's death in 1925 and served in the Senate until 1947, having lost his bid for reelection in 1946 to Joseph McCarthy.)

Although labor made concessions, it won a significant victory. The bill eliminated the hated, ineffective RLB and replaced it with Boards of Adjustment and a National Board of Mediation. The new law did not clearly articulate how the Boards of Adjustment were to be created, which was an obvious weakness. The act stipulated that the carriers and labor were to negotiate all disputes, and if an agreement could not be reached it was to be submitted to the Board of Mediation. Each party was to choose representatives without outside interference. If they did not request the assistance of the Board of Mediation, it could proffer its services, as the RLB did during the wage controversy. If an agreement could not be reached, the board was to refer the dispute to a new body, the Board of Arbitration, whose members were also to be appointed by the president. Rulings from this board were to be submitted to the U.S. District Court. Each party had ten days to file a petition to impeach the finding; if they did not, it became final, and the court had the power to enforce the order. This was a significant change because for the first time a ruling was to have some teeth. Having the board's rulings carry the authority of the federal courts—while perhaps not ideal—was better than allowing the courts to intervene with injunctions. Permitting courts to enforce rulings eliminated one of the most glaring weaknesses of the RLB. As a last resort, and if the dispute threatened to disrupt essential traffic in any section of the country, the Board of Mediation was to notify the president, who at his discretion could create an Emergency Board to investigate the quarrel. The Emergency Board was to issue a report within thirty days. During the investigation, and for thirty days after the president received the report, neither side could make any changes in pay or work conditions without mutual consent.[45]

The *Brotherhood of Locomotive Engineers Journal* offered perhaps the most insightful comment on the RLA: "The most significant fact about the Railway Labor Act is that the majority of railway executives have decided to quit fighting the railway unions and recognize them as a vital part of the industry."[46] Other publications also grasped the significance of the RLA. When the president signed the bill into law, a *New York Times* editorial described it as an all-important first step toward establishing cooperation between labor and management.[47] In an earlier editorial the paper argued that the bill " . . . may be epoch-making."[48] *Railway Age* recognized that not all railroad companies approved of the RLA, but urged labor and management to abide by its provisions.[49]

Conclusion

The six-year battle that the unions waged had finally paid off. The RLA was a pioneering measure. It established collective bargaining in the railroad industry a decade before that right was generally recognized. The right of railroaders to organize, granted before it was to other American workers, attests to the unique position in the national economy that they held and the belief that they deserved special legislative consideration.[50]

The rhetoric of industrial democracy was not used as frequently as it was immediately after the war, but the *Engineers Journal* invoked it again after the bill's passage. *BLEJ* stated that the law did not mean that unions were no longer needed,

But it does mean that the unions can now turn their attention to larger things and become more valuable than ever to their members, winning for them the rights of industrial democracy so that they may be something more than cogs in a great transportation machine.[51]

Clearly, to the unionists, passage of the Railway Labor Act meant more than just the right to organize. Its passage allowed the leaders of the unions to focus on more than bread-and-butter issues; they could become agents of members' advancement beyond the workplace.

Through the ballot box, and through *Labor* and other union publications, organized labor influenced the national debate about legislation in a way that previous generations of workers could not. Unlike some of their erstwhile allies in the progressive camp—and especially those even further to the left —the labor leaders were a pragmatic group whose main concern was to help their constituents. They were not interested in larger questions of political philosophy or the polemics of radicals. The labor leaders understood that to achieve their ends they could not be closely associated with radicalism. The Republicans, in 1924, wrote a labor plank that accommodated railroad labor. As both major parties have done at various times in American political history, they adopted a component of the opposition's agenda as their own, in an attempt to thwart their rivals. Railroaders were helped by their important economic position and by the desire of politicians to avoid potentially damaging strikes.

The RLA left many key issues unresolved. It sanctioned the independent brotherhoods' collective bargaining rights. The rights of nonoperating employees were seemingly expanded, but that was not clear in 1926. The RLA made the Boards of Adjustment mandatory, as the unions wanted, but it did not specify their scope, and the parties could not agree on their jurisdiction. The carriers wanted them created on a regional or system basis, and labor wanted them to be national in scope. No penalties were imposed if the boards were not created, and thus few were. The law did not clearly prohibit company unions. Some of the shortcomings of the RLA were soon to be addressed by the courts, which ultimately strengthened the law for unions.

Strengthening the Railway Labor Act

During the progressive era, industrial leaders came to rely on the national government to act as a stabilizing force in the economy.[1] Railroad labor and management expected that the RLA would have a similar effect. Yet because the law contained major shortcomings, the unions continued their activist tactics to gain stronger legislation. The Great Depression slowed the unions' efforts, but in 1934 Congress enacted amendments that reconstituted and strengthened agencies created by the RLA. The pro-labor character of Congress during the first New Deal seized the initiative from labor. In 1926, labor and management cooperated to write the legislation, but in 1934 the government's proposal prevailed, partly because internal disagreements weakened the railroad labor coalition.[2]

The weaknesses of the RLA were quickly apparent: it was ambiguous on the employees' rights to choose representatives to bargain with carriers, and it did not specify the jurisdiction of the Boards of Adjustment or make their formation mandatory. However, it took the unions eight years to secure revisions. Initially, they were reluctant to act because they did not want to alienate their political allies. The onset of the Great Depression created other, more pressing concerns for labor, carriers, and political leaders.

Several years of operation revealed other weaknesses. The president, in the opinion of the RLEA, loaded the Board of Mediation with second-rate men. Labor believed that President Coolidge made it " . . . a dumping place for deserving capitalists and defeated Republicans."[3] To labor, the appointment of Samuel E. Winslow of Massachusetts as chairman of the Board was a travesty. As a congressman in 1924, he was responsible for not letting the Howell-Barkley Bill come to the floor for debate. The carriers and the unions asked Coolidge not to appoint men from the defunct RLB, yet he appointed former RLB members Edwin P. Morrow and Glossbrenner Wallace William Hanger. Morrow's appointment, labor believed, had been pushed on Coolidge by Kentucky Senator Richard Ernst solely to eliminate a potential rival. The unions approved of Carl Williams, who edited *Farmer-Stockman*, an Oklahoma-based publication. He resigned after several months, and the president appointed former Texas Governor Pat Neff, known for his anti-labor policies. The final member of the original board was Hywel Davis, a friend of James Davis, secretary of labor. He died in January 1927, and the president appointed John Williams, who was less friendly to labor.[4]

The most important challenge to the RLA came in 1927 when the Brotherhood of Railway and Steamship Clerks, Freight Handlers, Express, and Station Employees (BRSC) filed a suit against the Texas and New Orleans Railroad. The carrier would not permit employees to choose representatives as specified in Section II of the RLA, which made it the duty of carriers and their employees " . . . to exert every reasonable effort to make and maintain agreements . . ." and to reach settlements so that service would not be interrupted. Labor won an important victory when the U.S. Supreme Court ruled in favor of the union.

Political Activities

Union leaders recognized the inherent weaknesses of the RLA and were dissatisfied with Coolidge's appointments, so it was inevitable that they would continue to pursue nonpartisan political action. As the 1926 election approached, *Labor* asked in a headline: "What Have You Done To Spread the Gospel?" The "gospel" was nonpartisan political action. To bolster circulation in the months leading up to the election, the paper offered a special rate of fifty cents for six months.[5] Because of limited financial resources, the RLEA focused most of its political energy on defeating unfriendly senators. Union publications, however, often published lists of RLEA-endorsed candidates for other offices as well.

The election gave labor the opportunity to support one of its most recent champions, Alben Barkley of Kentucky, who was running to unseat the incumbent GOP senator, Richard Ernst. As was its practice, *Labor* distributed special editions to support Barkley. Meanwhile, Ernst passed out issues of a bogus labor paper, which is an indication of the influence of organized labor. Barkley won handily and *Labor* boasted: "Does organized labor know how to

Figure 7. This figure celebrates a more politicized electorate and was a warning to GOP politicians prior to the general election of 1926.

'elect its friends and defeat its enemies?' Ask Senator Richard P. Ernst, senior senator from Kentucky. **He knows**."[6] [Bold in original text.] Barkley served in the Senate until 1948 when he became President Truman's running mate. After serving as vice president, he returned to the Senate in January 1955 until his death the following year.

Labor and other progressives also trumpeted the victory of David I. Walsh in Massachusetts's senatorial race. That race held special significance because of the importance President Coolidge placed on it. The president urged Bay State voters to support the incumbent William Butler, whom he called a great statesman and a friend of the administration. In every speech, according to *Labor*, Butler claimed his defeat would be a repudiation of the president. Walsh, who lost the 1924 race by 18,598 votes, defeated Butler by approximately sixty thousand votes. After the election Walsh sent a telegram to *Labor*'s editor, Edward Keating, and credited railroad labor for his victory.[7]

Butler's defeat carried added importance because he was chairman of the Republican National Committee, a post he resigned after the election.[8]

Smith W. Brookhart of Iowa returned to the Senate after the 1926 election. In 1924 he won a close and controversial victory over Democrat Daniel Steck. Brookhart angered much of the Republican establishment with his blistering attacks on both President Coolidge and his running mate Charles Dawes. Brookhart was initially declared the winner with 755 more votes out of nearly 900,000 that were cast. Steck, with the help of many Iowa Republicans, challenged the results. A Senate committee ordered a recount which ultimately declared Steck the winner. The Senate voted 45–41 to seat Steck in April 1926. Brookhart immediately returned to Iowa to face Senator Cummins in the upcoming GOP primary.[9]

Although many issues affected the elections in 1926, labor took full credit for the victories of candidates it endorsed. The *BLEJ* proclaimed: "Labor wielded a sharp political tomahawk in the national election . . . Labor defeated reactionary Republican Senators and elected Progressive Republicans and Democrats in Kansas, Massachusetts, Wisconsin, Iowa, Arizona, New York, and Oklahoma." The publication also reminded its readers that since La Follette's death no one had been willing to lead the progressives, and it urged senators to take a greater leadership role.[10] *Labor* also claimed that the poor showing in the mid-term elections ended the president's quest for another term, although Coolidge claimed he never intended to seek a second full term. When all the dust had settled, the GOP maintained slight congressional majorities, but could not rely on progressives to respect party lines.

As the Democratic and Republican conventions approached in 1928, the RLEA sent its legislative subcommittee to both conventions. RLEA Chairman David B. Robertson wrote to Bert M. Jewell, of the RED, that the unions' general counsel, Donald Richberg, would accompany the delegations " . . . and do whatever possible to prevent the nomination of such men as [Vice President Charles] Dawes by either party." He advised Jewell that he believed both parties had more respect for the political influence of labor than ever before, and, "I further believe that we can accomplish something by capitalizing on this particular situation at the sessions of the two old conventions."[11] It is, of course, difficult to gauge exactly how much influence labor had in 1928. Nonetheless, the comments are revealing; they demonstrate that labor leaders thought their organizations were powerful.

Railway labor approached the upcoming GOP convention with two principal concerns: first, that Vice President Dawes would not get the nomination; second that it would secure a favorable labor plank. Richberg, with Jewell's help, wrote a labor plank and presented it to Herbert Hoover, who approved it and submitted it to the Platform Committee without revealing the authors.[12] The final GOP platform included several important points contained in the labor proposal: most notably, that labor should have the right to bargain collectively. The platform endorsed the " . . . right to collective bargaining by free and responsible agents of their own choosing."[13] The ambiguity of the RLA on the issue of collective bargaining made the language of the platform especially important to the unions. The party platform also acknowledged that the use of court injunctions in labor disputes was a serious problem that might require further legislative action. It added that while the present railroad laws were based on sound principles, changing conditions might warrant amendments.[14] One of the points in the labor proposal that was not adopted was its call for labor relations in other industries to be patterned after the principles of the RLA.[15]

Shortly after Hoover received his party's nomination, he asked labor leaders to meet with his campaign advisers. The candidate did not attend, but his advisers tried to convince the RLEA to endorse Hoover. The executives were reluctant, but selected William N. Doak, vice president of the BRT, as temporary liaison with the campaign. As the election approached, Hoover embraced more conservative elements, which alienated progressives such as Richberg.[16]

Until the Democrats nominated a candidate, organized labor was reluctant to support Hoover. The Democrats eventually nominated Alfred Smith. Their platform also adopted favorable labor planks such as the right to bargain collectively. They also opposed the application of anti-trust laws to industrial relations, and advocated strict guidelines for the use of injunctions against strikes. Earlier in the year, Smith had supported a state measure, the Byrne-Lefkowitz Bill, which would have forbidden injunctions during a strike except after a hearing with both sides represented. As his party's presidential candidate, Smith made it clear that he would support legislation that would advance the working people of America.[17]

Given Smith's political record and the Democratic platform, it is somewhat surprising that the RLEA voted to remain neutral in the presidential election. It is not exactly clear why labor did not support Smith, although one can speculate that, like many Americans, they were leery of his Roman

Catholicism, his status as a wet, and his urban/immigrant roots. Labor organizations may have also been reluctant to support Smith if they believed that
Hoover would be the winner. In addition, while the Democratic platform
may have been more favorable, the GOP program was also quite positive.

Railroad labor remained active politically, endorsing congressional candidates solely on their labor record. Edward Keating, editor of *Labor* and one of
labor's most articulate champions, believed that 1928 was a "banner year" for
railroad unions' electoral activities. Eighteen of twenty-two senatorial candidates whom labor backed won. In several bitter primary battles, organized
labor helped such favorites as Robert La Follette Jr. (WI), Robert B. Howell (NB), Hiram Johnson (CA), and Lynn Frazier (ND) to victory. All four
Republicans won their respective general elections. Other labor-endorsed
candidates who won Senate seats in November included Henry Ashurst (D-
AZ), Henrik Shipstead (FL-MN), Burton K. Wheeler (D-MT), Key Pittman
(D-NV), and Clarence Dill (D-WA).[18]

Problems with the Railway Labor Act

While the RLEA geared up for another round of nonpartisan political activities, it also began to work to implement and revise the law. The RLA's most
serious deficiency was the ambiguity of the language regarding the creation
of Boards of Adjustment. The labor executives assigned the task of establishing boards to local officials, but gave them little guidance about how to proceed and, of course, the carriers were, at best, reluctant to cooperate. In many
cases the carriers simply ignored the requests to create boards.[19] The lack of a
uniform system of Boards of Adjustment created nationwide problems. If a
dispute was not solved it could be submitted to the Board of Mediation, but
only through a union's chief executive; the RLEA did not want locals pre-
senting cases directly. The board often refused to hear cases that came from
systems that did not have Boards of Adjustment. The number of unresolved
disputes mounted, and unions became increasingly frustrated because parties were not required to mediate disputes.[20] Like the RLB, the new system
was drowning in too many local cases.

Eventually, nearly three hundred system-based Boards of Adjustment were
established. Still, unions were not happy because system-based boards tended to destroy uniformity in labor agreements. Unions and carriers named
the same number of representatives to the boards; consequently many votes

ended in a tie.[21] Clearly, the dispute-resolution machinery left much to be desired. Instead of helping to solve the myriad of labor problems, the new system often only muddied the waters further.

The RLA granted workers the right to choose representatives, but carriers often frustrated unions by refusing to recognize duly elected men. While the unions preferred to focus on the language that granted them the right to choose their own representatives, management preferred to concentrate on the section that stated that any dispute resolution that was mutually acceptable to both parties was permissible.[22]

By early 1928, weaknesses in the law were becoming too serious to ignore. In January, as the Clerks' case was winding its way through the judicial system, the RLEA took the first tentative step toward revising the RLA. It created a committee to draft amendments that addressed the deficiencies in the law applicable to the creation of Boards of Adjustment. The RLEA also instructed the committee to draft stronger language protecting the right of workers to choose their own representatives without interference from the carriers.[23]

By March 1928, the committee, assisted by Richberg, had drafted two amendments to Section 1 of the RLA. The aim of both amendments was to strengthen employees' rights to choose representatives. The RLEA intended to weaken the foundation of company unions by trying to warn all employees of their employers' obligation under the Railway Labor Act. The proposed amendment stated:

> Every carrier shall notify its employes [*sic*] by printed notices conspicuously posted at such times and places as shall be specified by the Board of Mediation, that all disputes between the carriers and its employes will be handled in accordance with the requirements of this Act; and in such notices there shall be printed verbatim, in large type, the provisions of the second and third paragraphs of this section, which provisions thereby shall become part of the contract of employment between the carrier and each employe and shall be held binding upon the parties, regardless of any other express or implied agreements between them.[24]

The primary issue was management's interference with labor's right to choose representatives. The RLA stated that labor and management had the right to choose representatives to carry out negotiations without interference from the other party. Both groups often found it impossible to agree on who had been rightfully chosen, and carriers insisted on dealing with company union officials. The second amendment, also added to Section 1, granted the Board of Mediation the power to investigate the representatives whom the workers had elected. The board was to investigate the dispute and submit its report to the carriers within thirty days. During that period the board had the right to hold secret elections or to utilize any other appropriate method of ascertaining the names of the duly designated and authorized representatives of the involved parties.[25] Richberg wrote a third amendment to create a mechanism to enforce the new amendments. After other union leaders suggested additional amendments, the RLEA requested that each organization solicit suggestions from locals as well. The RLEA notified the Board of Mediation of its action, in part seeking further suggestions.

Judicial Help

As the RLEA drafted amendments to submit to Congress, a major legal battle unfolded between the Texas and New Orleans Railroad (T&NO), a subsidiary of the Southern Pacific Lines, and the BRSC. In 1926, with a wage dispute case pending before the Board of Mediation, the carrier undertook the formation of a company union, known as the Association of Clerical Employees–Southern Pacific Lines. H. W. Harper, general chairman of the BRSC on the carrier, appealed to the federal courts for an injunction because the company " . . . had endeavored to intimidate members of the Brotherhood and coerce them to withdraw" from the union.[26] The BRSC argued that the carrier's action interfered with the workers' right to select their own representative as specified by the RLA. In August 1927, Federal Judge J. C. Hutcheson Jr. issued a temporary injunction ruling that the union could organize without company interference; it became permanent the following April.[27] The ruling put company unions on very tenuous footing.

Judge Hutcheson's ruling did not end the clash. The road kept its clerks' association in operation and dismissed workers it suspected or knew to be involved with the BRSC. It also appealed Hutcheson's decision. The Fifth Circuit upheld the injunction by a 2–1 vote, and the case moved to the United States Supreme Court.[28] Writing for the majority, Chief Justice Charles Evans Hughes upheld the lower court's ruling, noting that the company violated the rights of employees to choose their own representatives and that it violated congressional intent, which was to prevent the interruption of interstate commerce. He wrote, "Freedom of choice in the selection of representatives on each side of the dispute is the essential foundation of the statutory scheme."[29] The decision added teeth to the RLA and, labor believed, dealt a severe blow to company unions. The Supreme Court did not give unions a new legal identity, but, following other precedents, it considered unions to be one among many possible organizations that could represent workers.[30] The verdict was a warning, shot over the collective bows of the carriers, that unions had to be considered legitimate bargaining agents.

The Supreme Court decision was one of the most significant labor rulings prior to the New Deal. While not outlawing company-run unions, it opened the door to further challenging their legitimacy. The *Engineers Journal* editorialized that the decision was of the " . . . greatest significance for railroad labor." Union General Counsel Donald Richberg declared that it meant that employers could no longer arbitrarily control the terms of employment and that employees were entitled to take their grievances to court to seek equity. Yet because of deteriorating economic conditions, the judgment did not mark the beginning of a drive to eliminate company unions. The BRSC acted independently in the case, and the RLEA became involved only in the latter stages. The association had had a difficult time focusing its energies on amending the RLA, and the case helped it to both clarify its stance and reinvigorate its efforts.[31]

The principle reason for the RLEA's lassitude was the Great Depression. By the early 1930s, the economic situation posed a bigger threat to railroaders than the weaknesses of the RLA. In early 1930, the president called a conference of labor and business executives to discuss the crisis, and later, in November, the RLEA met to formulate its own relief program. Establishing the six-hour day to fight unemployment was the first point of labor's eleven-point legislative agenda, which the RLEA unveiled in January 1932. The association also sought pensions and guaranteed work for one year. The final point called for observance of the spirit and intent of the RLA, including prompt disposition of grievances.[32] The AFL proposed a program that was similar to the RLEA's, but the two organizations failed to coordinate their actions and, thus, lost an opportunity to fully utilize their combined strength to influence national policy.

The various legislative maneuvers took place against a backdrop of rapidly declining traffic. Freight traffic reached a record high in 1929 when the nation's Class I carriers transported more than 1.3 million tons. By 1932 freight traffic was cut approximately in half to 646,223 tons. Between 1929 and 1933 the nation's railroads endured a 50.8 percent reduction in revenue from operations, which they helped to offset by reducing their payrolls by 50.1 percent, mostly through layoffs. Approximately 750,000 railroad workers lost their jobs. In 1926 the number of passengers was 874,000,000, but in 1933 the figure was less than half—434,848,000.[33]

To help economize, the carriers asked their employees to voluntarily accept a 15 percent wage reduction. In 1931, several major companies, including U.S. Steel, General Motors, U.S. Rubber, Pittsburgh Coal Company, and Ford Motors, announced wage reductions.[34] Following suit, the RLEA and the carriers negotiated a 10 percent wage reduction effective January 1, 1932. Labor agreed to the reduction because they thought it would create more jobs.[35] By 1933, railroad employment had declined by 41.5 percent from 1929 levels. The Baltimore and Ohio was the one exception to the trend of furloughing workers during the early years of the depression. Daniel Willard, president of the B&O, ordered that a placement service be created to help employees who were forced to accept part-time employment or who were laid off. Additionally, and more significantly, he ordered that one thousand boxcars, one thousand heavy gondolas, and forty-five locomotive tenders be built; most of the work was to be completed by B&O employees. As a result, between January and October 1930, the number of B&O shop craft employees rose 1.4 percent. Their principal competitors cut their shop employment: the Pennsylvania 8.4 percent, New York Central 8.5 percent, and the Erie 11.3 percent.[36]

The Reconstruction Finance Corporation, created in 1932, gave a temporary boost to railroads and other enterprises but did nothing to improve the structural causes of the railroad's problems. The Great Depression was the immediate cause of the industry's woes, but the corporate structure of the carriers had long been suspect. Arguments over valuation of stock and the true value of the carriers stretched back for decades. For just as long, corporate barons had managed to stave off any real action that would have addressed these significant problems. Finally, it was a large group of insurance companies, along with Harvard, Yale, Columbia, and the University of Chicago, that commissioned a study to survey the problems and, if possible, recommend solutions. Serving on the study committee were President Calvin Coolidge, who died before it issued its report; Barnard M. Baruch; *Atlanta Constitution* editor Clark Howell; International Harvester president

Alexander Legge; and former New York Governor Alfred Smith. The report, written by Harold G. Moulton of the Brookings Institute, recommended that railroad executives cooperate to voluntarily reduce expenses; that metropolitan terminals be consolidated; that financial management be improved; that methods and equipment be modernized; and that regulatory jurisdiction be extended to the entire national transportation system. The study group discussed the condition of labor at length, but did little except to note that railroad wages had not kept pace with those in other industries.[37]

The Hoover Administration left office at about the same time that the committee issued its report. President Franklin Roosevelt's message to Congress on May 3, 1933, concerning the nation's transportation crisis contained key elements of the Moulton report. Subsequently, the Emergency Transportation Act of 1933, which passed Congress at the end of the Hundred Days, contained many elements of the report. The act's principal purpose, to help carriers operate more efficiently, was similar in design to the National Recovery Act. President Roosevelt appointed Joseph B. Eastman to the new post of federal coordinator of transportation. Union officials feared that the push for greater efficiency would eventually cost jobs. Eastman admitted as much during congressional testimony, so they successfully lobbied to amend the act so that he could not lay off more workers. The amendment established the number of railroad employees in May 1933 as the baseline.[38]

In the autumn of 1933 the RLEA, prompted by passage of the Emergency Transportation Act and the increasing dissatisfaction with the Railway Labor Act, renewed its efforts to amend it. The RLEA sent questionnaires to all organizations seeking their suggestions. Some union leaders suggested that labor abandon its long-held position that National Boards of Adjustment should be created and settle for a compulsory system of regional boards that would have the authority to resolve disputes.[39]

The RLEA, now chaired by BRT President Alexander F. Whitney, was not the only group seeking revision. Oscar B. Colquitt, a member of the Board of Mediation, suggested amendments to clarify the duty of the board to proffer its services in individual grievance cases where no adjustment board had been created and to provide for the appointment of a neutral umpire, agreed upon by the parties or appointed by the Board of Mediation, when the Board of Adjustment deadlocked. Colquitt had an appointment with Roosevelt to discuss the issue, and sought Whitney's opinion on the amendments before

Figure 8. Alexander F. Whitney, BRT president and leader of the RLEA during the push to enact railroad pensions. By permission of the United Transportation Union.

the meeting, but Whitney said he would have to discuss the proposal with the entire association.[40]

Early in 1934, the Legislative Committee of the RLEA met with FDR to discuss possible amendments to the RLA. FDR passed them on to Eastman. The unions, however, prepared the amendments without the coordinator's counsel and persuaded Representative Robert Crosser (D-OH) to introduce them on February 5. Crosser was from Cleveland, so he represented many railroaders. The proposed amendments would have strengthened labor's position in four areas. The unions sought to reinforce their bargaining power by stipulating that the representatives chosen by the employees did not have to be employed by the carrier. They also wanted the Board of Mediation to have the power to hold secret elections to determine the rightful representatives of the employees. The unions proposed fines of up to $20,000 and jail sentences for parties who refused to comply with the law. Finally, Crosser's bill called for the creation of a National Adjustment Board, which the unions had sought since 1920.[41]

As an alternative to the Crosser Bill, the administration offered its own amendments, written by Eastman and introduced by Senator Clarence Dill (D-WA) and Representative Sam Rayburn (D-TX). Both men had helped Eastman write the Emergency Transportation Act. The Dill-Rayburn Bill contained several key differences. One sentence drew labor's ire: "The majority of any craft or class of employees shall have the right to determine who shall be the representative of the craft or class for the purposes of this act." Labor argued that such language strengthened company unions. Union executives, Whitney most vocally, opposed language that prohibited employers from forcing workers to join or not to join a labor organization, and stipulated that any existing percentage agreements were to be voided.[42] Whitney opposed both clauses because, he argued, they would destroy the existing percentage agreements that the BRT had on a number of roads " . . . which contemplate that in the employment of new men in train or yard service, a certain percentage shall be members of our organization."[43] Labor's opposition carried little weight. The version signed by FDR on June 21, 1934, contained the objectionable language.[44]

The amendments forbade any limitations on the form of association among employees and provided for prompt settlement of disputes concerning rates of pay, rules, and working conditions.[45] They also made it more difficult to maintain company unions because employers could no longer collect dues, fees, assessments, or other contributions to labor organizations. In an attempt to give the law some teeth, failure to comply with it was made a misdemeanor, punishable by a fine or imprisonment. Another important victory for the labor organizations was that it won its long fight to create a National Board of Adjustment (NBA), which was to be composed of thirty-six members; carriers and labor would each appoint eighteen members. The NBA, patterned after the boards that operated during World War I, was to be divided into four sections, each handling grievances of a specific class and operating independently of the other sections.[46] Further, the amendments abolished the Board of Mediation and created in its place the National Mediation Board (NMB), its three members appointed by the president. Either party could invoke the NMB's services in disputes concerning proposals to change rates of pay, rules, or working conditions not adjusted by the parties. If the NMB failed to effect a settlement it was to convince the parties to arbitrate the matter.[47]

Generally, the amendments were a positive step for organized labor, but the RLEA was no longer politically unified. The railroad labor executives did not follow Whitney's lead in opposing the amendments, which he believed would be extremely detrimental. The other union leaders were willing to accept the amendments, even though they did not agree with all the proposals. The unity that had marked the relationship between the labor organizations was clearly strained when T. C. Cashen of the Switchmen's Union of North America threatened to take the BRT to court if it opposed the bill.[48]

Further evidence of the break became apparent as the midterm elections approached in 1934. Whitney urged railroaders to vote against Crosser, whom he charged with helping to kill the six-hour bill and supporting an open-shop clause in the RLA. The legislative committee of the RLEA disagreed with Whitney's assessment. In a carefully prepared statement, the committee wrote that it feared it would be charged with dereliction of duty if it did not set the record straight. Its statement then refuted each of Whitney's charges and concluded with a ringing endorsement of the Cleveland-area congressman. The BRT's own National Legislative Representative J. A. Farquharson signed the letter.[49] Crosser was reelected.

Conclusion

The split in the ranks of labor was significant. Since the formation of the Plumb Plan League in 1919 the unions had presented a united front. Even if labor executives disagreed privately, their disputes were never aired publicly. The split within the RLEA over the amendments and Crosser's reelection ended fifteen years of cooperation. Thus, the 1934 amendments to the Railway Labor Act mark the end of an era of union-initiated legislation. Although Crosser introduced labor's bill, the wishes of the Roosevelt Administration ultimately prevailed.

Passage of the RLA was the high-water mark of railroad labor's political unity and influence. Between 1926 and 1934 the ability of unions to influence elections declined. They could not win amendments to the RLA or continue their experiments in cooperative enterprises. The decline of railroad employment was only part of the explanation. Growing animosity between labor leaders and fading memories of the war years and industrial democracy also contributed to the decline. During the 1920s, the federal government acted to facilitate cooperation between the unions and carriers, but the New Deal also transformed the government into an active participant in labor issues. By 1934, the government had usurped labor as the catalyst of labor legislation; the desires of the unions were subordinated to those of the federal government.

Railroad Retirement and Social Security

As the Great Depression deepened, revising the Railway Labor Act of 1926 was just one of the objectives of the brotherhoods. Simultaneously, the RLEA argued that changing conditions warranted industry-wide, federally sponsored retirement insurance.[1] They argued that developing a national pension scheme would establish a safer, more efficient transportation network, and that guaranteed pensions would entice older workers to retire, allowing furloughed men to return to work.[2]

The RLEA's efforts to enact retirement legislation further weakened the once-powerful union alliance. Conflict arose, in part, because a group of disgruntled railroaders calling themselves Railroad Employees National Pension Association (RENPA) challenged the RLEA. The weakening of the RLEA, coupled with the resurgence of the AFL as a result of the National Recovery Act, allowed the Federation to briefly reassert itself as the principal voice of American labor. The Congress of Industrial Organizations in the mid-1930s eclipsed both the AFL and the railroaders.

The Railroad Retirement Act (RRA) of 1934 was an important forerunner to the Social Security Act.[3] Accounts of the creation of the Social Security Act, however, generally ignore the groundbreaking nature of the RRA.[4] Labor leaders who helped to write the RRA also had a hand in shaping national Social Security legislation.[5] Its enactment helped to resolve troubling constitutional issues, the most important being the legality of Congress establishing a mandatory pension system. The willingness of the government to assert authority evinces its changing role in economic stabilization and the growing link between workers and the state. Pension legislation brought order to an area formerly distinguished by chaos. Early pension plans were generally inadequate, disjointed efforts by various groups aimed at supporting the growing number of elderly Americans.

Labor executives found allies among those who had worked to enact state pension laws in the 1920s.[6] The most important ally was Senator Robert Wagner (D-NY), who wanted railroad retirement legislation created because of its wider implications. Retirement insurance had long been of interest to Wagner. The Great Depression furthered his desire to create a national pension system for railroad workers, whom he believed fell under federal authority to regulate interstate commerce. Railroad pensions would provide a " . . . laboratory for experiment . . ." and " . . . blaze the way for full treatment of the problem."[7] The *Brotherhood of Locomotive Firemen and Engineers Magazine (BLFEM)* told its readers: "It can easily be seen . . . what important precedents it [the Railroad Retirement Act] is intended to set, and what constitutional questions and questions of public policy will be involved."[8]

History of Old-Age Pensions

The idea of old-age pensions first gained popularity during the progressive era because demographic and technological changes altered the American landscape.[9] Advances in science and medical knowledge helped increase the average life expectancy from forty to fifty-six between 1850 and 1920.[10] The faster pace of work and the increased risk of injury created a greater need for retirement insurance; men found it increasingly difficult to work until death. New technology also contributed to the demand for pension benefits, as older workers often found it difficult to adapt. Hoping to increase morale and efficiency, some companies introduced pensions. Most Americans remained opposed to the dole, but many realized the necessity of a carefully planned, dignified method of meeting the basic needs of the millions of elderly Americans.[11]

The number of older people in the country grew rapidly. Between 1900 and 1930, the number of people over fifty-five years of age increased from 7.12 million, or 9.3 percent of the total population, to 15.18 million, or 12.3 percent of the population, which had grown from slightly more than 76 million to approximately 123 million. Statistics compiled by the Association for Improving the Condition of the Poor revealed that between 15 and 20 percent of Americans over sixty-five were wholly or partially dependent upon others for support.[12]

Before 1929, forty-seven pension bills were introduced and defeated in Congress.[13] Early proposals varied except on one important point: only the most destitute would be eligible.[14] After World War I, a determined group of social reformers began to promote pensions. The Fraternal Order of Eagles (FOE), along with the United Mine Workers (UMW) and the American Association of Labor Legislation, spearheaded this movement. The FOE hired Abraham Epstein, who previously worked for the Pennsylvania Old Age Commission, as its chief advocate. The FOE lobbied at the state level, and eventually drew up the "standard bill." It maintained the principle that only the poorest should receive benefits. It allowed a maximum benefit of $1 a day provided the recipient was at least seventy, had resided in the state for fifteen years, possessed property valued at less than $3,000, and had no other means of support. The underlying principle was to maintain the family unit by extending to the needy individual a money grant, which the FOE considered the simplest, most economical method of assistance.[15]

The FOE and Epstein worked tirelessly, but with little success; only six states enacted pension laws between 1923 and 1927. The statutes were not mandatory as the FOE advocated. In most states, the Eagles found it necessary to support measures that made counties mostly responsible for funding and administrative problems. Only in Montana did a majority of counties approve a pension measure, which allowed 673 persons to collect benefits. The most significant contribution of the FOE was to educate the public, which gradually shifted its attitude away from the ideals of individualism, familial support, and luck.[16]

By 1929, four more states and Alaska had enacted pension statues. By 1935, eighteen more states and Hawaii had passed pension laws. The measures were relatively uniform, usually patterned after the standard bill: each had a residency requirement of ten to twenty years; a recipient had to be between sixty-five and seventy; all applicants had to prove that they were in need and had no close relatives who could help; and owning property of a specified value, usually about $3,000, could disqualify a person. If qualified, recipients received a small stipend, generally $25 to $30 a month. A few states, such as Kentucky, where the United Mine Workers worked diligently to enact the legislation, set an annual maximum of $250. Although the number of recipients was small—perhaps 3 percent of people over sixty-five—some Americans received state pensions.[17] Those lucky few owed a debt to Epstein and the FOE. Still, many deserving elderly could not receive pensions.

Many business leaders and corporate executives opposed pensions—government-sponsored or otherwise. Opponents who believed that pensions would increase expenses found fast allies in the National Association of Manufacturers (NAM) and many Chambers of Commerce. Shippers and farm organizations opposed railroad pensions because they believed rates would be increased.

Corporate and Union Pension Programs

Not surprisingly, the scope of company-run pensions remained narrow. The welfare capitalism movement of the interwar years prompted some corporations to recognize the importance of employee pensions. Employers were driven to create pensions less from generosity than their desire to instill self-reliance in their corporate families. As historian Nikki Mandell writes, "They preferred to stimulate the work ethic by rewarding industriousness over the long run rather than rewarding hard work in the short run."[18] Between 245 and 310 businesses operated pensions by 1925 that covered between 2.8 million and 3.5 million workers—still a fraction of the population. By 1929, approximately four hundred companies offered pensions, covering approximately four million workers. Between 1929 and 1932, according to figures compiled by the Industrial Relations Counselors, Inc., almost 10 percent of the retirement plans had been discontinued. During the same period, plans covering approximately 1.1 million workers were reduced.[19] In 1933, less than 15 percent of the American workforce received pensions.[20]

Even if an employee worked for a firm that offered a pension plan, collecting the benefits could be difficult. The corporate pension programs fell into one of four categories: discretionary, limited-contractual, contractual, and reduced labor. A discretionary plan provided a pension to an employee who reached a certain age and had been with the company a specified number of years. The employer, however, could determine the payment and change the terms, or even abolish the program. About three-quarters of the retirement plans in the country fell into this category.

Under a limited-contractual plan, which covered about 25 percent of workers with pensions, the employer could not alter a retiree's payment. This arrangement was of little benefit to men still working, because the company maintained the right to alter or amend its plan at will. The third system bound the company and the employee to a plan that could not be altered, but few workers had such plans. Industrial pensioners averaged a yearly payment of slightly more than $500.[21]

A fourth, albeit informal, retirement scheme occurred when companies gave older workers a less demanding job as reward for years of faithful service.[22] Some pensions were little more than discretionary awards requiring a working retirement. Firms used them to force retirees to return to work if their services were required, such as during a strike or other labor problem. As Frank Vanderlip of National City Bank noted, a worker who collected a pension often " . . . would sacrifice much of his personal liberty, including his right to strike for better wages or shorter hours."[23]

Compared to private-sector workers, government employees had greater access to pensions. Retirement plans for firemen and police officers were practically universal, and teachers' pensions were common. Some three hundred thousand federal civil servants received pensions under the Sterling-Lehlbach Act.[24]

Railroad Retirement Plans

When the government federalized the nation's railroads, thirty-nine carriers operated pension programs. The Baltimore and Ohio Railroad initiated the first railroad pension in 1884. It established sixty-five as the standard retirement age, and based payment on a percentage of the operatives' daily wages, usually between 20 and 35 percent.[25] The dawn of the new century saw one of the nation's largest firms, the Pennsylvania Railroad Company, establish a pension program, and six years later the Atchison, Topeka and Santa Fe Railroad (ATSF) followed suit. The Pennsylvania required operatives to retire at seventy, or sixty-five if they were disabled. Pensions were based upon 1 percent of the recipients' monthly pay during their last decade of employment.[26] The ATSF offered retirement benefits to any employee who, at age sixty-five, had fifteen years of continuous service, or any employee who became physically unable to work. Benefits ranged from $20 to $75 monthly, and "special cases" could receive up to a 25 percent bonus. The program did not cost the workers anything.[27] By 1932, fifty-one Class I carriers operated pensions. Besides the B&O, Pennsylvania, and ATSF, some of the major carriers that offered pensions included the Chicago and Northwestern Railroad, the Union Pacific, the Chicago, Burlington, and Quincy Railroad, and the New York Central Railroad.[28]

Some unions operated pensions or offered other benefits to retired members. If unions offered pensions it was in one of four forms: lump sum superannuation benefits, permanent and total disability benefits, homes for the

Figure 9. Residents and guests of the ORC Retirement Home, Christmas 1929. The ORC was one of several unions that provided assistance beyond pensions for retired members. By permission of the Kheel Center for Labor Management Documentation and Archives, ORC and Brakemen, Collection, Cornell University.

aged, or monthly pensions.[29] Of these, monthly pensions grew most steadily prior to the Great Depression. By 1930, approximately 28 percent of the trade unionists in the United States and Canada belonged to organizations that offered pensions.

Some unions imposed strict rules of eligibility. Of the ten international unions with pensions, four required recipients to be members for twenty years, two required twenty-five years of membership, and another required thirty years of membership. The unions typically prohibited men from entering the pension department after they had reached a certain age, usually forty-five or fifty.[30] Given the fluid nature of railroad employment, especially prior to World War I, few operatives could qualify for pensions. Like many other pension schemes, most union plans were not created on sound actuarial practices.

The elderly of America were covered by a patchwork of old-age pension systems. Most Americans, according to Maxwell Stewart, believed that ambition, thrift, and hard work would suffice. He called Americans' belief in the sanctity of thrift the "spell of the frontier."[31] Historian Christine Stansell argues that the idea of benevolence, philosophically elaborated by a variety of eighteenth-century thinkers, made humanitarian charity part of a broad-minded, cosmopolitan Anglo-American sensibility of the following century.[32] These two views contain elements of the American system as it existed prior to the Great Depression, but it was clear by 1929 that the system—or lack of one—no longer met the changing needs of society.

RLEA Involvement

On the eve of the Great Depression, the RLEA began to take an interest in pensions. It addressed the pension question in the spring of 1929 and appointed Alexander F. Whitney of the BRT, P. J. Conlon of the International Association of Machinists, and D. W. Helt of the Brotherhood of Railway Signalmen to investigate the pension question. That autumn the AFL endorsed government-sponsored pensions.[33]

Pressure from the RENPA, rather than a firm conviction that pensions were needed, prompted the RLEA into action. W. W. Royster, a BLE state official in Minnesota, created the RENPA in 1929, which took the lead and forced the RLEA to play catch-up.[34] This small group of displeased workers played a critical role in helping to forge important links between American workers and the federal government. The primary political concerns of the RLEA were to revise the Railway Labor Act and to adopt the six-hour day—that is, until the RENPA retirement plan made it to the halls of Congress.

In March 1930, the RLEA endorsed the concept of state and federal pensions. It opposed any system funded by employee contributions. The most meaningful action the RLEA took was to instruct Donald Richberg to prepare a legal summary of the pension question that stated what was clear to everyone: creating railroad pensions through federal legislation involved difficult questions for which there were no handy precedents.[35] As its floundering actions indicate, the RLEA had no clear vision of a retirement program and was not moving with the decisive assurance that marked its efforts to create the Plumb Plan League a decade earlier.

As the Great Depression deepened, existing pension funds struggled to stay afloat. As early as 1925, the *BLEJ* warned that many pension funds were troubled. Although the article had not meant to imply that the engineers' fund was one of the troubled funds, rumors inevitably began to circulate.[36]

To meet the potential crisis some international unions tightened restrictions and increased the age of eligibility.[37]

Pensions operated by carriers were also troubled. Payments were usually drawn from current revenues, which worked well if earnings remained high and pension costs relatively low. This arrangement, however, was contrary to sound actuarial advice, which asserted that the best funding method was for employees to deposit a small amount from each check over their careers into an interest-bearing account. Until 1928, the Interstate Commerce Commission (ICC) prohibited carriers from establishing plans as recommended by actuaries. By then revenues were already declining, and carriers could not afford to establish the necessary cash reserves.[38] By 1932, aggregate pension payments increased from slightly more than $2 million in 1908 to more than $30 million.[39] By the early 1930s, the pension obligations were too large to ignore. Other corporate pension funds were also troubled.[40]

Unlike the flat-footed RLEA, RENPA drafted a plan which, like many contemporary schemes, was hastily drawn up and gave little or no thought to long-term solvency. Its principal objective was to prompt older workers to retire so younger, furloughed men could return to work. Critics, including independent actuaries and the Carnegie Foundation, argued that while the plan might offer a short-term fix, ultimately it would fail to establish a sound retirement system because it did not create adequate cash reserves.[41]

The brotherhoods ignored RENPA, although it was becoming increasingly difficult. BLFE president David B. Robertson did not respond to a request from Royster to address a RENPA meeting in the autumn of 1931. In a September 1931 article in *The Railroad Trainmen*, BRT President Whitney told readers not to participate in RENPA activities. He wrote that any organization that condemned the leaders of bona fide labor unions was not a true friend of railroaders. The following year he warned members that if they were involved with RENPA, they could not hold a union office.[42]

Snubbed by labor leaders, Royster took the proposal to Washington. In a remarkable show of faith—or an extraordinary demonstration of naiveté—he wrote all 531 members of Congress requesting their assistance; he found few sympathetic ears. One senator willing to listen was Smith W. Brookhart (R-IA), a maverick who was a favorite of the brotherhoods.[43] Brookhart introduced the bill the same day that he met with Royster. Two days later, however, he withdrew it, telling Royster that he could not sponsor it because the railroad unions, to whom he said he owed a great deal, opposed it.[44] After

Figure 10. Labor unions frequently urged members to write their legislators to support union agendas. The unions supplied a form letter the members were to follow. While imagining the capitol, this man urges his representative to support the Railroad Retirement Bill.

Brookhart withdrew it, Royster met with other legislators, including Representative Robert Crosser (D-OH). After more than a week of discussions with Royster, Crosser decided not to introduce the bill, citing his relationship with President Robertson of the BLFE.

It was at this point, according to Royster, that he met with Representative Kent Keller (D-IL). Keller, who represented a mining district, was not afraid to upset the brotherhoods. He agreed to introduce the measure because he wanted to establish a government-sponsored retirement system for miners too. In the Senate, Royster convinced Senator Henry Hatfield (R-WV) to introduce the bill. Hatfield had received a great deal of positive correspondence from his constituents who worked for the Chesapeake and Ohio Railroad even before Royster approached him. He told Royster that if he got a similar response from Baltimore and Ohio workers, he would sponsor the legislation. Royster claimed that within ten days Hatfield got more mail from B&O operatives than he had previously received from C&O employees.[45]

Pension Legislation Introduced

Pension supporters hoped to avoid the discord that would occur if carriers and unions began to cut or eliminate pensions. Concurrently, they hoped to improve sagging morale by ensuring workers' financial stability. Declining revenues led to massive layoffs, increasing the average age of those operatives who remained.[46] Many contemporaries believed that the federal government should step in with some kind of regulation to ensure the solvency of various pension programs. Businessmen, although they often opposed pensions, could not argue with Senator Wagner when he maintained that a retirement fund would also preserve safety and efficiency in the railroad industry.[47] Henry R. Corbett, a consulting actuary who helped the RLEA draft its proposal, wrote:

> The admitted need of some old age retirement provision is shown by arguments found everywhere in business journals, in programs of business organizations, in the special reports on this subject promulgated from time to time by chambers of commerce, manufacturers' associations and trade organizations like the Metal Trades Association.[48]

Wagner and Crosser introduced the RLEA-sponsored plan on March 2, 1932; several days after Representative Keller introduced his RENPA-backed bill.[49] The purpose of the Wagner-Crosser Bill was to increase safety and efficiency in interstate transportation. It would accomplish these goals by encouraging workers to remain in the industry and rewarding workers for years of service, as well as promote safety and improved service by giving operatives benefits they would not receive in other industries.[50]

Although supporters of retirement insurance had laid a solid foundation, the legislation had little chance of passing in 1932. Groups such as the Chamber of Commerce and the National Association of Manufacturers were among the most vocal opponents. Carriers objected to pensions, like their allies, because of the cost, and they argued that it would hurt efficiency, because operatives would be able to move freely between employers without fear of losing their pensions.[51] Eventually, the carriers dropped their opposition as part of an informal agreement they reached with the RLEA when the two parties were negotiating a 10 percent wage decrease.

Robertson wrote, in the *Brotherhood of Locomotive Firemen and Enginemen's Magazine*, that the chiefs' bill had been carefully researched with the best actuarial and legal advice, while the other proposals had not.[52] The RLEA-sponsored legislation called for the creation of a reserve fund that would be adequate well into the future. RENPA refused to respond to Robertson's charge that its plan was unsound. Not surprisingly, Donald Richberg, testifying before a congressional subcommittee in favor of the RLEA plan, which he helped to create, charged that the framers of the RENPA bill based it on the pay-as-you-go principle, and the government would soon be forced to rescue it.[53] An actuary, William R. Brieby, also testified and agreed with Richberg.[54]

Perhaps more importantly, constitutional controversy beset the proposals. Questions arose because it was not clear that the legislation fell within the purview of the commerce clause of the Constitution. Closely related to the issue of constitutionality was a larger question: should the federal government pass legislation that dramatically altered its responsibilities to so many Americans?

The struggles that Abraham Epstein and the Fraternal Order of Eagles waged to enact state pensions, and the lukewarm reception that they received, revealed deep-rooted opposition. To many Americans, government-sponsored pensions were closely associated with socialism. The Great Depression altered the political landscape. Pro-pension forces gained an important ally in Franklin Roosevelt who, as governor of New York, supported state pensions.[55]

The pension bills died in committee in both 1932 and 1933. The following year Wagner and Hatfield reconciled the differences between their bills and introduced their compromise bill in the Senate.[56] In the House, Keller and Crosser introduced the new proposal separately. These bills were the basis for the Railroad Retirement Act of 1934. In one important feature the 1934 version differed from previous proposals: the preamble stated that its purpose was to relieve unemployment, not improve efficiency. Hatfield claimed that its passage would allow one hundred thousand aged workers to retire and would permit the immediate hiring of an equal number.[57]

Many congressmen supported the bill, and the president gave his tepid approval.[58] As the debate unfolded, it became apparent that many, like Senator Wagner, viewed the bill as a precursor to more far-reaching federal retirement legislation. On the Senate floor James J. Davis (R-PA) stated, "I think it is reasonable to pioneer in this field in connection with the railroad industry because so many excellent improvements in our social and industrial life have been made possible through it." Wisconsin's Thomas O'Malley echoed that sentiment in the House.[59]

The Senate Interstate and Foreign Commerce Committee reported the bill favorably. One can only imagine what Wagner, Hatfield, RENPA, and the leaders of the RLEA thought on June 14, 1934, when the retirement bill passed the Senate 66–0.[60] Its most significant features included compulsory retirement at sixty-five, provided the operative had worked five years, or after thirty years of service; each operative would pay 2 percent of his monthly compensation into the annuity fund, an amount that his employer would match; his retirement compensation was to be computed by multiplying 2 percent of his average monthly income by the number of years of service; and the legislation created a three-man board to administer the program.[61]

The Railroad Retirement Bill passed in the House in only slightly different form, and the Joint Conference Committee quickly resolved the differences.[62] President Roosevelt signed the bill into law on June 28, although not without reservations. A statement released by the White House said: "The bill, although improved in its final form, is still crudely drawn and will require many changes and amendments at the next session of Congress."[63] The influence of Transportation Coordinator Joseph Eastman was evident in the statement. He did not oppose the idea of pensions, but he objected to the bill in its current form. He urged that action be delayed so further studies could be completed.

As expected, opponents challenged the bill immediately. Chief Justice A. A. Wheat of the Supreme Court of the District of Columbia ruled late in October in favor of the more than one hundred Class I carriers who had brought the suit. In his decision, Wheat ruled that Congress could pass pension legislation that covered employees engaged in interstate commerce; however, the Act went beyond that by covering workers who were employed in intrastate commerce. He also faulted it because it permitted any person who left a carrier, for whatever reason, within one year prior to the passage of the act, to be eligible for an annuity. If there was a bright spot for labor in the ruling, it was that he made it clear that he was not ruling that Congress had no right to pass a retirement bill, only that in its present form it was unconstitutional. The Retirement Board continued to meet under the assumption that the United States Supreme Court would overturn the ruling.[64]

Labor remained optimistic as the battle moved to the Supreme Court. However, it upheld the lower court, 5–4. The majority attacked the legislation with gusto, arguing that the bill was an attempt to create social legislation and therefore did not fall under congressional authority under the commerce clause of the Constitution. The court ruled that the taxing mechanism took the carriers' property (money) without due process, and confirmed the lower court's ruling that workers not engaged in interstate commerce were covered by the law.[65]

The minority opinion, written by Chief Justice Charles Evans Hughes, stated that the gravest aspect of the majority decision was that it denied Congress power to pass any compulsory pension act for railroad employees. He argued that the majority paid insufficient attention to the obligations that carriers had to their employees, responsibilities that the minority believed could not be confined to the contractual engagement. The principal argument of the minority was that there was little distinction between compensation given to workers injured through no fault of the employer, and fair recompense for years of service. Hughes contended that the underlying principle was that Congress had the power to tax the nation's transportation system as a unit for the purpose of regulation as long as particular properties were not subject to confiscation. That principle, he noted, had been upheld many times.[66]

Within two weeks of the ruling, Crosser and Wagner introduced a new bill. The mechanics of the pension system remained largely unchanged. The underlying philosophy had been subtly altered, however. Framers based the new legislation upon congressional power to tax, not its power to regulate interstate commerce.[67] The second Railroad Retirement Act implied that all employees could be covered because they all were subject to federally imposed taxes. Actually, two bills were submitted separately. The first bill established the machinery of the railroad retirement system, and the second bill—in theory unrelated—authorized a tax on the pay of railroad operatives and the payrolls of the carriers, to be paid into the U.S. Treasury. The formula used to compute the taxes was essentially unchanged from the overturned retirement law. President Roosevelt signed the measure into law on August 29, 1935.

Conclusion

Retirement insurance proponents learned valuable lessons from the failed retirement legislation. The U.S. Supreme Court ruled that the commerce clause did not give Congress the authority to establish pensions, which compelled proponents to base the bill on congressional authority to tax. The press covered the debate that surrounded the Railroad Retirement Act, which educated the public.

There is little doubt that Social Security would have become law even without the Railroad Retirement Acts of 1934 and 1935. The railroad acts, however, established the precedent of Congress passing national retirement legislation. The Supreme Court's ruling that overturned the Railroad Retirement Act of 1934 illuminated faults and helped framers of the Social Security Act to avoid similar mistakes. The experience gained from the controversy surrounding the RRA ensured that the Social Security Act would have an excellent chance of withstanding the inevitable legal challenge.

Railroad Unions and Labor Banks

By 1919, the term *industrial democracy* was firmly established in labor's lexicon, and it animated its political activity.[1] As explained in the previous chapters, railroad labor vigorously pursued industrial democracy through the ballot box in the interwar years. Railroad unions, particularly the Brotherhood of Locomotive Engineers through its banking ventures in the 1920s, pursued a second course to achieve industrial democracy or, perhaps more accurately, financial democracy. In 1920, the BLE founded its first bank, and until 1927 it was at the forefront of a small but vigorous effort to establish labor banks. Proponents argued that banks should cater to the needs of working Americans, help them to obtain credit more readily and enable them to purchase stock. The BLE argued that labor banks would move unions' battles from the picket line to the board room.[2] This chapter of labor history has been largely ignored by recent historians.

Examining trade unionists' banking venture is essential to understanding their effort to define their place as citizens in an industrial democracy. The railroaders valued political action, but looked upon labor banks as a second, critical component in their campaign to establish industrial democracy. They believed that financial equality was a necessary step on the path to full citizenship in an industrial democracy. Union leaders had long recognized the paradox of putting unions' money and the savings of workers into traditional banks, where it could be loaned to businesses and possibly used against labor. The goal of labor banks was to help union members obtain loans and credit more readily, which would permit workers to advance individually and as a group. Leaders hoped that a new class of industrialists would emerge with the help of sympathetic banks.

The railroad leaders were not the first American workers to turn to labor banks. In 1810, members of New York City's General Society of Mechanics and Tradesmen founded the Mechanics Bank. Like the BLE a century later, the Mechanics hoped to help members obtain credit more readily. This was not a smooth process. After a brisk start, within two years " . . . plagued by mismanagement of its investments . . ." the directors were forced to declare temporary insolvency.[3] The bank nonetheless survived and helped to ensure that the city's " . . . credible mechanics . . ." had fair access to financial accommodations.[4] Although the rhetoric of the railroad leaders was different in the twentieth century, the desire to break away from the grip of financiers was unchanged.

BLE President Warren S. Stone was a dedicated banking proponent. He divided labor history into three epochs: the beginning of class-consciousness and organization, the general struggle for collective bargaining, and the era of cooperation with employers rather than war. Stone believed that labor banks would help to create the last era.

Labor banking enthusiasts argued that credit was one of workers' principal needs and asserted that because most banks were reluctant to extend either credit or loans to working people, workers were denied a fair chance to advance. One of the chief architects of the labor banks was Stone, who argued that one of the principal tasks of labor banks was to be responsive to the needs of working Americans. Stone believed that labor banks would help to end conflicts between employer and employee. BLE Assistant Grand Chief William B. Prenter summed up the union's position:

> In America there is no such thing as a working class as distinguished from a capitalist class. Men pass too readily from one group into the other to be tagged with class labels. It is the Brotherhood's aim in its financial enterprises to show its members and workers generally how they can become capitalists as well as workers.[5]

Antecedents of Labor Banks

Prior to the twentieth century, some labor organizations dabbled with the notion of labor banks, but with little success. The AFL discussed the possibility of creating banks at their 1904 convention, but decided against further action. In 1912, the BLE rejected a banking resolution. At its next triennial convention in 1915, however, the brotherhood instructed Stone and the Advisory Board " . . . to consider the advisability of forming a bank at an opportune time."[6] World War I foiled any immediate plans the brotherhood may have had, but the Advisory Board continued to gather information and in October 1919, it authorized Stone and Prenter to draft a banking plan.

Several factors came together following the war that made the atmosphere ripe for banking. The unions applied the phrase "make the world safe for democracy" to industry as well. The term "industrial democracy" came into vogue in the United States, and workers believed that the principles of democracy should be applied to the workplace.[7] The *BLFE Magazine* used the language of war propaganda: "There is not one factor that will contribute more effectively in 'making the world safe for democracy' than the democratization of the financial system of the United States." Banks, the article noted, could be the greatest institutions of service or oppression, depending upon how they were operated.[8]

Additionally, the government's pro-labor policies strengthened railroad unions and helped their membership to rise to record levels, which filled their coffers. During the war, many Americans purchased government bonds, learning for the first time that money could be invested in securities that paid a higher yield than savings accounts. Increased wages also meant that for the first time many working people had discretionary income.[9]

Corporate leaders launched an open shop drive after the war, which prompted the BLE to act. By 1921, the various open shop groups had come together under the banner of the American Plan. They mobilized to destroy the "un-American" closed shop. Trade unionists believed that the formation of labor-controlled banks would help them thwart the open shop drive.

In one instance a labor bank helped end a strike, which became an example often cited by unionists as a portent of the potential power of labor-controlled banks. In the summer of 1920, the unions involved in the Norfolk, VA, shipbuilding industry demanded higher wages. In retaliation, the companies demanded an open shop, which led to a strike. The owners of the Crescent Machine Company renounced its membership in the employers' association, however, and acquiesced to the union's demands. As a result, it did quite well financially. Other shipbuilding companies demanded that Crescent's bank block the firm's credit. The bank consequently demanded the immediate repayment of the firm's outstanding debts. The unions involved in the strike appealed to a newly formed workers bank, the Mount Vernon Savings Bank of Washington, DC, which was associated with the International Association of Machinists. Mount Vernon declared its readiness to guarantee Crescent's credit, thus enabling the company to honor all the terms of the agreement struck with the unions. Labor leaders quickly grasped the significance of the victory; Stone went so far as to claim that it meant the end of strikes.[10] It would not be the last time that Stone engaged in overblown rhetoric.

The nation's cooperative movement was another impetus for the banking movement. In America cooperatives had a long history, and were usually associated with agriculture. In the 1830s cooperatives were seen as a way to uphold customary production practices and provide artisans with competences. By the 1880s, proponents viewed cooperatives as a way to "republicanize" industry.[11] Farmers in Minnesota and Wisconsin ran nearly five thousand cooperative societies of various kinds in the early 1920s. Trade unionists reasoned that if farmers and industrial workers could operate cooperatives, they could run banks too. The *Brotherhood of Locomotive Firemen and Enginemens Magazine* told readers that if workers and farmers used their economic power cooperatively they could own banks all over the country. The magazine advised its readers that " . . . legitimate banking is safer, more easily managed than a co-operative store or factory."[12]

Many unions were interested in the possibilities cooperatives offered. At its 1919 convention in Denver, the BLFE passed a resolution urging cities to establish municipally owned markets and cold storage houses. This resolution, aimed at the beef trust, had no political effect but indicated labor's interest and faith in cooperatives. The *BLFE Magazine* ran a regular column dealing with the benefits of cooperation. The Maintenance of Way Employees Union purchased textile plants in Michigan and Ohio to manufacture knit goods, underwear, gloves, and other clothing.[13]

Enthusiasm for the cooperative movement in the twentieth century reached its apex in early 1920 when the All-American Farmer-Laborer Co-Operative Convention convened in Chicago, symbolically on the anniversary of Abraham Lincoln's birth. Grand Chief Engineer Stone told delegates that every dollar saved in a labor bank could be used to benefit working Americans. In retrospect, it is clear that Stone, while well-intentioned, was extremely cavalier. He said:

> You know there is something wrong, and we have been led to believe . . . that there are only a chosen few of the world's anointed that can understand the mysterious thing we call Finance. Before we get through we are going to show you, by some of the best speakers and the authorities in America, that it is the easiest thing in the world [to operate a bank]. We are going to put in a system whereby the farmers and the workers and those who need the small savings to build improvements, can have a system of banks of their own.[14]

Delegates approved a cooperative commercial and banking plan to protect the public from what delegates thought to be an exploitative capitalistic system. They stated that labor should organize its own press, and that working Americans should follow the example set by the Maintenance of Way Employees in establishing cooperative enterprises.[15] An overly optimistic editorial writer of *Labor*, probably its editor, Edward Keating, hailed the results of the convention as " . . . a new Emancipation Proclamation."[16] The enthusiasm generated by the convention soon dissipated, however, because there was no overall coordination.

In June 1920, union officials finalized the union's banking plans. A letter to the BLE membership, which appeared in the August 1920 issue of the *Brotherhood of Locomotive Engineers Journal* explained that banking had been thoroughly researched, and that it was entirely safe. The union chartered BLE National Co-Operative Bank as a national bank. One million dollars of stock was to be sold for $100 per share and was available only to BLE members. The new bank opened on November 1, 1920, across the street from the brotherhood's headquarters in downtown Cleveland.[17]

Stone served as president of the bank and Assistant Grand Chief Prenter, secretary-treasurer of the union, became its vice president and head cashier. Walter F. McCaleb, former vice chairman of the Dallas Federal Reserve Board and a labor banking advocate, assumed the post of vice president and manager. Union members made up the bank's board of directors.[18] With the exception of McCaleb, the new institution's leadership had no banking experience, which proved to be a costly mistake. Operating banks was not as easy as Stone thought.

Growth and Expansion

Initially, the bank flourished. Fueled by fear of the open shop drive, and thoroughly versed in the language of the cooperative movement and industrial democracy, BLE members quickly deposited their savings in the bank. Two months after it opened, the BLE Co-operative National Bank had more than $1 million on deposit. Six months later deposits exceeded $7 million, and the rapid growth attracted national attention. Steady growth continued, and by 1924 deposits exceeded $26 million.[19]

Other unions, noting the success of the BLE's bank, were anxious to found their own financial institutions, and scores of requests for information poured into the BLE. Unionists had to be convinced why their organization should not open a bank, rather than why it should. McCaleb of the Engineers' Bank addressed the 1921 convention of the Order of Railway Telegraphers, extolling the virtues of labor banking. It is impossible to measure his influence, but the Telegraphers voted to establish a bank, which opened on June 9, 1923.[20]

About a year after the formation of the Cleveland bank, the BLE undertook an expansion program that can be attributed to genuine rank-and-file enthusiasm. (See Table 1) Banks were not founded in a community until local unionists expressed an interest; at that point the BLE would intervene.

Table 1. The BLE's Financial Institutions

Cleveland, OH	November 1920	Merged with non-labor bank, 1930
Hammond, IN	November 1921	Sold, May 1926
Nottingham, OH (Cleveland)	April 1922	Sold, June 1929
Minneapolis	December 1922	Failed, Great Depression
Spokane, WA	August 1923	Liquidated, Jan. 1929
New York City	December 1923	Sold, August 1926
Boston	May 1924	Interest maintained
Portland, OR	January 1925	Interest maintained
Birmingham, AL	February 1925	Lost control, 1927
Hillyard, WA	February 1925	Liquidated, Jan. 1929
Philadelphia	April 1925	Sold, May 1927
Tacoma, WA	July 1925	Interest maintained
Seattle	August 1925	Lost control, May 1929
San Francisco	December 1926	Sold, February 1929

Source: *The Labor Banking Movement*, 46–47, 281–344.

EUROPE

$695 SEVEN WEEKS TOUR $695

Including all expenses.   Hotel and steamer accommodations first class

LEAVE MONTREAL JULY 13 ON THE NEW CANADIAN LINER MONTLAURIER

LONDON	YOUR BANK will personally conduct this tour. A great opportunity to see MORE OF EUROPE FOR LESS MONEY than you had ever dreamed.	ENGLAND
PARIS		SCOTLAND
ROME	Make your reservations now. Applications limited to sixty.	HOLLAND
VENICE		BELGIUM
THE HAGUE	YOU WILL SEE MORE IN THESE FIFTY-TWO DAYS THAN THE AVERAGE TOUR IN EIGHTY DAYS.	FRANCE
BRUSSELS		GERMANY
MUNICH		ITALY
THE ALPS	*Write today to the* TRAVEL BUREAU	SWITZERLAND

Brotherhood of Locomotive Engineers Cooperative National Bank

308 Euclid Avenue   WARREN S. STONE, President   Cleveland, Ohio

Figure 11. In addition to running banks, the BLE sponsored trips to Europe. The union believed that industrial democracy would be achieved through a financial system operated by unionists for the benefit of workers.

Generally, the union left the formation of the bank to the Brotherhood Investment Company, a newly formed $10 million subsidiary corporation of the BLE that provided a majority of the investment capital and selected the directors from among local BLE members or the officers in Cleveland. Again, it should be noted that the union often appointed unqualified men to policy-making positions. In 1924 and 1925 the union established a series of regional and state security corporations, which it used to maintain a majority share of the stock in its various banks.[21]

Increasingly, Chief Stone's monthly message to members in the *Journal* dealt with financial issues. He warned the membership—prophetically as it turned out—that wildcat schemes cost investors hundreds of thousands of dollars annually. Generally, the union advised members of the safest investments and assured them that it would look out for their best interests. By the middle of the decade, a regular column appeared that advised engineers on investments. Other financiers, so the argument went, were more concerned with lining their own pockets than with helping the engineers achieve financial security.

In the early 1920s, it might have seemed to the BLE that they were well on their way to ushering in an era of industrial democracy. When they expressed class-consciousness, it was not that of the working class, but rather that of the middle class. The success of labor banks reflected the engineers' changing perception of themselves. Stone's admonitions to save money were revealing. He argued that members would be able to obtain things formerly available only to people of the upper middle class, and that labor banks were largely responsible for helping to democratize society. He wrote, "You want them [your children] to get the best that a good college has to offer."[22] It is striking that in 1923 a labor leader mentioned sending the children of trade unionists to college. The BLE bank also sponsored European trips.

While Stone and the union leadership encouraged members to invest their money in safe, sound securities, the BLE itself developed a diverse portfolio. Among the union's growing ventures was a large investment in the Equitable Life Building in New York City, the largest office building in the world, and Park Lane Villa, a luxury apartment building in Cleveland. Stone reportedly rented an apartment in the building for $1,100 a month. A group of engineers, led by Stone but independent of the BLE Bank and the union itself, owned the Coal River Collieries, a series of coal mines in Kentucky and West Virginia.[23] Advertisements announcing the sale of stock in the Coal River Collieries or other undertakings appeared regularly in the *BLEJ*, and Stone encouraged the membership to invest in these enterprises in his monthly column.[24]

The number of labor banks peaked in 1926 when thirty-six banks had $108,899,264 in deposits. Between 1920 and 1926 the Amalgamated Clothing Workers; the New York State Federation of Labor; the American Flint Glass Workers; the International Ladies Garment Workers; the Brotherhood of Railway and Steamship Clerks, Freight Handlers, Express and Station Employees; and the International Printing Pressmen and Assistants' sponsored or owned banks.[25]

Gathering Storm

At the top of the BLE financial network stood Warren S. Stone, a former engineer on the Chicago, Rock Island and Pacific Railroad, who had never been east of Chicago until he assumed the position of Grand Chief Engineer in August 1903 when P. M. Arthur died. Stone was born Feb. 1, 1860, in Iowa. Unlike many of his generation, he graduated from high school and attended college. He began his railroad career in 1879 as a fireman on the Rock Island Railroad. He fired until he became an engineer in 1884. While an engineer he served as secretary-treasurer and head of the Grievance Committee of his local division. Later he served as chairman of the Central Committee of Adjustment for the entire Rock Island system.[26]

To many workers, Stone symbolized a new age. Sidney Hillman of the Amalgamated Clothing Workers, an enthusiastic supporter of labor banks, considered Stone " . . . one of the master builders of the American labor movement."[27] Many unionists would have agreed with Hillman's assessment.

Ironically, Stone, as president of the Coal River Collieries, refused to recognize the United Mine Workers, touching off a raucous debate with John L. Lewis.[28] Perhaps from Stone's perspective as head of a powerful union that most carriers recognized, collective bargaining was a certainty and conflict at a minimum, but clearly that was not the case for most American workers.

Stone, who suffered from Bright's disease, was hospitalized for two weeks in April because of illness. A diabetic whose health had been failing, Stone aggravated the condition by working many hours. On June 9, 1925, Stone collapsed in his office and died three days later. The following week, *Labor* mourned his death, calling him an "organizing and financial genius."[29] One of the monuments to his "genius" was the brotherhood's nationwide banking chain, but Stone's death was a turning point in the history of labor banking. While the phenomenon was at its height nationally, the BLE's own financial empire was on the verge of collapse.

By the time of Stone's death, mismanagement of the BLE financial empire had reached monumental levels. During his tenure, union credentials had always counted for more than banking experience in the selection of officials. The career of BLE member George O. Barnhart illustrates this point. In 1925 he had been a union member for forty-one years and had risen to become chairman of the General Grievance Committee of Adjustment on the Oregon, Washington Railroad and Navigation Company. He had no financial experience, yet he served as president of the Brotherhood Banks in Spokane, Portland, and Tacoma and was chairman of the board of the Pacific

Brotherhood Investment Company of Seattle. At the brotherhood's bank in Birmingham, AL, the union controlled eight of fifteen seats on the Board of Directors. All eight of the men appointed by the union were BLE officers or union members. Professional bankers, who generally considered the BLE banks pariahs, shied away from them.[30]

Labor banks, like all businesses, tried to cater to the particular needs of their clientele. One of the compelling reasons for the engineers to open banks was to help members to obtain credit more easily. The Amalgamated Clothing Workers' Banks pioneered small loan services ranging from $50 to $300, an area formerly controlled by loan sharks and pawnbrokers. The Amalgamated Banks also helped customers with small building loans and home mortgages. While the Amalgamated Banks were quite successful because they followed standard banking procedures, the BLE often placed more emphasis on a worker's character references rather than his ability to repay a loan. As a result of their credit-granting policy, BLE banks soon had a much larger number of bad loans than well-managed commercial banks. BLE banking officials too often spent an inordinate amount of time trying to collect on bad loans.[31]

The union's top-down management policy was a mistake, especially in the smaller banks. Too often a bank's officers were not from the community, and customers sensed their aloofness. The union moved personnel frequently, making it more difficult for bankers to become acquainted with customers. Because of this policy, many of the union's smaller banks, particularly those in the west, adopted a policy of concentrating surplus capital in investments rather than loans. Stone adopted this policy, partly because he hoped to strengthen the ties between labor and agriculture. Thus, for political reasons rather than sound business practices, the brotherhood banks were closely linked to the spreading agricultural depression.[32]

When confronted with the disturbing news about the bank's emerging crisis shortly before Stone's death, in May 1925, the union's Advisory Board had three options. First, it could call a convention to deal with it, which several members recommended. Stone vetoed that option. Another option was to regain economic stability through more conventional management. Third, the BLE could try a bold scheme to cover up the deficit and recover its losses. Unfortunately, the Advisory Board chose the final option. Influenced by George T. Webb, the union's "chief financial man," Stone and the others decided to invest money in the booming Florida real estate market.[33] The

BLE membership and investors in its firms learned of the board's decision, but not its motives.

In July, several weeks after Stone's burial in Cleveland's Lake View Cemetery, the brotherhood welcomed customers and guests to the opening of its new banking headquarters. According to the *Journal*, thousands of well-wishers from all corners of the continent streamed through the building, which the *Journal* called "one of the finest banking edifices in the country."[34]

While the bank's opening and Stone's death seemed like the major events of the summer, in retrospect, the decision by the leadership to recoup the lost money was the truly important event. Hoping to recover their capital quickly, the officers purchased thirty thousand acres of choice land in Sarasota County, FL. To develop the land, the union formed the Brotherhood of Locomotive Engineers Realty Company, capitalized at $1 million. Stone orchestrated the scheme in the final weeks of his life. On May 27, officers of BLE Bank signed an agreement that stated that the Brotherhood Investment Company would suffer no loss through exchanges of securities with the bank.[35] The agreement would later be the basis for the first in a series of lawsuits brought against the union and its financial institutions.

Venice, Florida

The Florida real estate market was one of the great speculative ventures in the twentieth century, and it reached its apex about the time of Stone's death. The rich had long sought refuge in the state's warm climate, but a number of changes occurred in the post-war years that made the state affordable and attractive to Americans of more modest means. These changes included the increased use of cars and increased road construction. Florida appealed to many people because it signified a revolt against urbanization and industrialization; Americans wanted to retreat to new and undeveloped places. Florida's real estate market improved gradually after 1921. Each winter more and more "snowbirds" loaded up their Model Ts and made the trip south. In the winter of 1924–1925, however, land speculation became rampant. The union sought to grab this golden ring.

The BLE began a large-scale promotional blitz to convince its members of the wonderful opportunities that awaited them in Venice, which the union hoped would become another Miami. The first hint of the impending Florida scheme appeared in the November 1925 issue of the *BLE Journal*. Editor Albert F. Coyle described Florida and how it had grown the previous few years, but he made no mention of the union's real estate investment.[36] A few months later, Harry J. Stuart, an engineer, wrote about his recent visit to Venice in a letter to the editor. He described the city as "nature's fairyland" with "sun-kissed bays." Venice, he wrote, was a lodestone that attracted thousands of tourists, and would soon be to the west coast of Florida what Miami was to the east coast.[37] It seems likely that the editors planted or perhaps fabricated the letter, but with such glowing descriptions from one of their purported peers, it is not surprising that the membership responded by opening their wallets when the union asked them to purchase stock in the Brotherhood Realty Company.

In the March 1926 issue of the *Journal*, the BLE officially announced that the union was going to develop a model city at Venice. It told readers that Venice would be one of the only cities in America where men of humble means could live alongside millionaires in neighborhoods surrounded by similar homes. In addition to articles in the *Journal*, members were deluged with multicolored circulars that proclaimed, "Come to Venice, the resort supreme on Florida's West Coast. There ten acres and independence await you."[38]

The tone of President Prenter's column in the April issue of the *Journal* indicates that some of the rank and file may have questioned the union's Venice venture:

> I want to say again that we acquired this property in Venice after long, careful, expert investigation; that we believe it is the finest piece of land for beautiful home sites and profitable farm development obtainable anywhere in Florida, and that we do not hesitate to recommend it to our members and their friends, not as a speculation, but as a sound investment in increasing value.[39]

The Advisory Board could not have chosen a less opportune moment to enter the Florida real estate market. By the time it decided to initiate the speculative venture in late 1925, the boom was already in decline. In August 1925 rumors circulated that the Internal Revenue Service would begin investigating profits from Florida land deals, and that speculators would have to report their entire profits from transactions in the year the sales were made, not just the portion that had been paid. Further, railroad lines into

Florida became overburdened and were in need of repairs. Also in August, the Florida East Coast Railroad announced an embargo and a permit system on carload shipments of all goods except fuel, petroleum, livestock, and perishable materials. Lack of warehouse space added to the rising problem; 851 rail cars sat still loaded in Miami.[40]

Fifth Triennial Convention

By the time the engineers gathered for their triennial convention in June 1927, the union was in deep trouble. There is little evidence to suggest that the delegates expected anything but a routine convention, although many engineers may have been suspicious, because the union had sold the Brotherhood of Locomotive Engineers Cooperative Trust Company in New York City in 1925 and the Brotherhood of Locomotive Engineers Title and Trust Company in Philadelphia just four days before the convention began. Most members likely thought their organization was the nation's leader of a small but growing revolution in the structure of the American economy. The convention opened amicably on June 6. Leaders estimated that it would take about three weeks for delegates to conclude all the union's business; it actually took six. Although few people understood it at the time, the convention marked the end of the BLE's banking movement.

Delegates quickly appointed a committee to unravel the union's financial network. Adrian Newcomb, a prominent local judge, chaired the so-called Committee of Ten. It spent the remainder of June and most of July wading deeper and deeper into the financial swamp. Its report became the basis for the union's financial restructuring, revealed gross mismanagement, and eliminated any illusions about the union's financial health.

Judge Newcomb told the convention delegates that the brotherhood was approximately $12 million in debt.[41] He submitted no formal report, but one member of the committee, D. G. Myers, estimated that the union's losses would be at least $19 million. Others suggested that when the losses of members were taken into account, the figure would be closer to $30 million.[42] One thing was clear: financial mismanagement had nearly ruined the union.

The Venice project was a staggering catastrophe. The membership thought that Florida offered a wonderful opportunity for investment, so funds poured into the new subsidiary company from the sale of stock to the membership,

Figure 12. When financial mismanagement destroyed the BLE's banking operations and nearly the union itself, it tried to raise needed capital through Loyalty Loans. Members did not buy enough bonds and so dues were increased.

pension funds, and the union's banks and investment companies. Eventually the union acquired fifty thousand acres, and began to develop a new model community. According to a report from the Fifth Triennial Convention, the union, through its banks and other financial institutions, invested at least $16 million in Venice, and the BLE membership added perhaps an additional $4 million. Construction of the Hotel Venice offers a vivid example of mismanagement. Developers estimated that the hotel would cost between $175,000 and $200,000. Unfortunately, it was built on a cost-plus contract, and, although the final statement was lost, investigators estimated that the total cost was approximately $638,000. BLE leaders hid the disaster in Florida from the membership through false financial statements and by issuing dividends—presumably paid for with money illegally borrowed from other union institutions. Judge Newcomb said that following the various transactions through the union's many companies made him dizzy.[43] BLE members who invested for "ten acres and independence" got something quite different.

Delegates learned that they would have to raise $7 million or more through a special assessment to ease the union's financial plight. To make matters worse, if that were possible, Judge Newcomb informed them that the membership could be held individually responsible for the union's bad investments. To cover this obligation, the union decided to take out second mortgages on its Cleveland properties. It also required all members to pay $5 monthly, in addition to their regular dues, for two years. Members received the option of purchasing interest-bearing Loyalty Bonds instead of paying the monthly assessment. The goal was to sell one hundred thousand Loyalty Bonds for $100 each within sixty days to raise $10 million and avoid the special assessment. Not surprisingly, the bonds did not sell rapidly, so the BLE had to levy the special charge.[44]

The BLE undertook several measures to reduce expenses. For one, it began to sell its assets. In addition, while it had previously paid each member's subscription to *Labor*, the convention voted to end that practice, thus saving approximately $48,000.[45] Since the formation of the Plumb Plan League eight years earlier, the railroad unions had cooperated closely on political issues, and *Labor* was their most important, articulate communicative link. By severing its ties to the paper, the BLE was also taking a step away from the other unions. Thus the BLE's financial trouble also weakened railroad labor's political alliance.

In response to charges that top leaders had been negligent, delegates voted to abolish the offices of president, first vice president, second vice president, and secretary, which saved the union an additional $52,000 annually, and the delegates hoped to force the office holders to resign. However, Prenter, L. G. Griffing, H. P. Daugherty, and C. E. Lindquist, who held the respective offices, refused to step down, which provoked charges by the convention that they had handled the brotherhood's affairs with " . . . laxity, carelessness and with indifference."[46] No outside witnesses or lawyers were present when delegates acted as jurors at the subsequent trials before the convention. Except for Prenter, who claimed to be too sick to attend, the others were found guilty and barred from holding office in the Grand Lodge for three years. Although not officially found guilty, Prenter resigned. Alvanley Johnston, the union's Grand Chief Engineer, became its chief executive. He was born in Ontario in 1875, and began working as a call boy for the Great Northern Railroad in North Dakota in 1892. He worked as an engineer between 1897 and 1909. Before being elected assistant Grand Chief of the BLE in 1918, he was general chairman of the Great Northern division of the BLE.

The sentences seem relatively light considering the extent of the malfeasance. The light sentences reflect the engineers' desire to keep negative publicity to a minimum. The full extent of the disaster was not reported in the *BLE Journal*, *Labor*, or the *Cleveland Plain-Dealer*, and neither local nor federal authorities charged the officials. Delegates placed the union's business and banking affairs in the hands of three trustees, S. H. Huff, J. C. McDermand, and A. O. Van Pelt, all high-ranking officials in the BLE or its related financial institutions, but not associated with the scandal.[47]

Conclusion

The BLE's banks ultimately did little to thwart the business interests of the 1920s or to further the ideals of industrial democracy. The lure of excess profits, personal gain, and in the case of Stone, national recognition, proved to be too much for top officials, most of whom lacked sufficient experience in the financial industry. The engineers' experiment in banking, however, illustrates their attempt to move beyond political activism and to strike at what they considered one of the roots of inequality—the nation's financial system.

The catastrophe came at an inopportune time for the brotherhood's political alliance. Stone and the BLE had led the alliance, but the debacle severed the once-strong alliance. Increasingly, leadership of the RLEA fell on other unions leaders. David B. Robertson, president of the Brotherhood of Locomotive Firemen and Enginemen, succeeded Stone as political leader. In the fight to enact the Railway Labor Act of 1926, the BLE took a less active role than it had earlier in the decade, and after 1927 withdrew further, which was a heavy blow to the labor coalition. The financial morass touched off jurisdictional contests for members between the BLE and BLFE, which further weakened the political alliance. Most engineers began their careers as firemen, but when they were promoted to engineer they could maintain their membership in the BLFE or they could join the BLE. The BLE tried to poach members from the BLFE because it needed the money their dues would add to its own coffers.[48] By the end of the decade the *BLE Journal* seldom carried political news; the union had lost the zeal and respect that it had once possessed.

Above all, the BLE's financial crisis symbolized the changing character of the union's institutions during the 1920s. Rather than a crusade for industrial democracy, the BLE's efforts became a failed campaign for middle class respectability and financial democracy.

Notes

Chapter 1. Introduction

1. Montgomery, *The Fall of the House of Labor*, 6.

2. Green, *The World of the Worker*, 100.

3. Hawley, *The Great War and the Search for Modern Order*, 2nd Edition, 5.

4. McCartin, *Labor's Great War*, 7.

5. Ibid., 224.

6. Fraser, *Labor Will Rule*, 118.

7. For a detailed study of the response of American women during World War I to the question of citizenship, see Jensen, *Mobilizing Minerva*.

8. Davis, *Power at Odds*, 1–3.

9. Fraser, *Labor Will Rule*, 128–129.

10. Ibid. Sidney Hillman of the Amalgamated Clothing Workers, communists, socialists, and other left-of-center political groups come to mind. Railroad unions had skillfully distanced themselves from these groups.

11. Cohen, *Making A New Deal*, 300–310.

12. Zieger, *Republicans and Labor*, 158.

13. *Labor* was originally called *Railroad Democracy* but the name changed shortly after publication began.

14. The AFL had forged close ties to the Democratic Party during the progressive era, especially during the Wilson administration, but after World War I the Federation's ties and influence had waned. See Greene, *Pure and Simple Politics*.

15. Huthmacher, *Senator Robert Wagner and the Rise of Urban Liberalism*, 177.

16. See Bernstein, *The Lean Years*.

17. See Olssen, "The Making of a Political Machine," 373–396; see also Zieger, *Republicans and Labor*.

18. Mink, *Old Labor and New Immigrants in American Political Development*, 17.

19. Clements, *The Presidency of Woodrow Wilson*, 73.

20. Fraser, *Labor Will Rule*, 127–128.

21. See, for example, Barrett, *Work and Community in the Jungle*; Davis, *Power at Odds*; Norwood, *Labor's Flaming Youth*.

22. Montgomery, *The Fall of the House of Labor*, 7.

23. See Dubofsky, *The State and Labor in Modern America*.

24. See O'Brien, *Workers' Paradox*; Zieger, *Republicans and Labor*.

25. See Bucki, *Bridgeport's Socialist New Deal*, who argues that state and local political issues helped to shape the specifics of New Deal liberalism. The groundswell from the state and local levels goaded national political leaders to respond. Also see Cohen, *Making A New Deal*; Brock, *Welfare, Democracy, and the New Deal*, 7–9. Brock discusses numerous examples of expanding state and local government responsibilities during the 1920s.

26. McCartin, *Labor's Great War*. McCartin chronicles labor's use of the rhetoric of the Great War, especially the phrase industrial democracy, as it tried to reshape its world; Bucki, *Bridgeport's Socialist New Deal*, 8.

27. Rayback, *A History of American Labor*, 114.

28. Zakson, "Railway Labor Legislation 1888 to 1930," 319.

29. Quotes from Huthmacher, *Senator Robert F. Wagner and the Rise of Urban Liberalism*, 176–177; Modlin, "Who Shall Support the Aged Worker?" *The Railroad Trainmen*, 46 (August 1929): 808.

Chapter 2. Railroading Prior to World War I

1. Licht, *Working for the Railroad*, 44–45.

2. Ibid., 44–46.

3. For an academic study see Stromquist, *Generation of Boomers*. For firsthand accounts see French, *Railroadman*; Brown, *Brownie the Boomer*.

4. McCaleb, *Brotherhood of Railroad Trainmen*, 38–47.

5. *Feeding the Iron Hog*, 12–19.

6. Ibid., 22–24.

7. Reed, *Forty Years an Engineer*, 32–33.

8. *Feeding the Iron Hog*, 17.

9. Seidman, *The Brotherhood of Railroad Trainmen*, 7.

10. Richardson, *The Locomotive Engineer, 1863–1963*, 352; Licht, *Working on the Railroad*, 131.

11. Seidman, *The Brotherhood of Railroad Trainmen*, 7; Richardson, *The Locomotive Engineer*, 352–353.

12. *Feeding the Iron Hog*, 29.

13. Licht, *Working for the Railroad*, 195.

14. David Lightner, "Labor on the Illinois Central Railroad, 1852–1900," (Cornell University: Unpublished Ph.D. dissertation, 1969), 263, cited in Licht, *Working for the Railroad*, 195–196.

15. Stover, *American Railroads*, 155–156.

16. Licht, *Working for the Railroad*, 182–183.

17. French, *Railroadman*, 15.

18. Licht, *Working for the Railroad*, 189–190.

19. Reed, *Forty Years an Engineer*, 20–21.

20. French, *Railroadman*, 80–84.

21. Reed, *Forty Years an Engineer*, 35; French, *Railroadman*, 180–181.

22. Robbins, *Railway Conductors*, 59–60.

23. The Brotherhood of Locomotive Engineers was founded in 1863; the Order of Railway Conductors, 1868; the Brotherhood of Locomotive Firemen and Enginemen, 1873; and the Brotherhood of Railroad Trainmen, 1883.

24. Robbins, *Railway Conductors*, 11; McCaleb, *Brotherhood of Railroad Trainmen*, 9.

25. Arnesen, *Brotherhood of Color*, 5–29.

26. By the early twentieth century, seven major railroad combinations dominated the United States. The Vanderbilt Roads consisted of the New York Central and the Chicago and Northwestern; the Pennsylvania Group included the Pennsylvania, Baltimore and Ohio, and the Chesapeake and Ohio; the Morgan roads were the Erie and the Southern; the Gould System included the Missouri Pacific; the Rock Island System was the Rock Island Road; the Hill roads were the Great Northern, Northern Pacific, and the Burlington; and the Harriman Roads consisted of the Union Pacific, Southern Pacific, and Illinois Central. See Stover, *American Railroads*, 148–149.

27. Ely, *Railroads & American Law*, 83–84.

28. Ibid., 84–85.

29. Richardson, *The Locomotive Engineer*, 241.

30. In the decade after 1877, the Knights of Labor were at their apex and they supported strikes in many industries, including railroads. In 1884, the Knights were involved in two strikes on the Union Pacific, and in 1885 they were involved in several strikes against the Gould lines. The Knights met defeat in a second walkout against the Gould carriers in the southwest in the spring of 1886.

31. See Zakson, "Railway Labor Legislation 1888 to 1930," 317–391.

32. Ibid., 320; Lecht, *Experience Under Railway Labor Legislation*, 23.

33. U.S. 25 Stats. 501 (1888). All references to this legislation refer to it as the Act.

34. Ibid; Zakson, "Railway Labor Legislation 1888 to 1930," 321–325.

35. Lecht, *Experience Under Railway Legislation*, 23; Richardson, *The Locomotive Engineer, 1863–1963*, 281–282.

36. Lecht, *Experience Under Railway Legislation*, 17–18; Richardson, *The Locomotive Engineer, 1863–1963*, 282–283; Zakson, "Railway Labor Legislation 1888 to 1930," 326.

37. Report of the U.S. Board of Mediation and Conciliation for 1913–1919, 24, cited in Lecht, *Experience Under Railway Legislation*, 26.

38. Richardson, *The Locomotive Engineer, 1863–1963*, 243.

Chapter 3. The Great War and its Aftermath

1. Stover, *Life and Decline of the American Railroads*, 122, 155.

2. Stover, *American Railroads*, 169–170.

3. Memorandum For Daniel Willard, president of the Baltimore and Ohio Railroad, prepared by John G. Walber, Vice President of Personnel, New York Central Railroad, undated, Herbert Hoover Presidential Library, Commerce Papers (Hoover MSS), Box 504, West Branch, IA; N. C. Harrison to Rep. William D. Upshaw (D-GA), July 12, 1921; Hoover MSS, Box 505; J. R. Browne to Herbert Hoover, January 18, 1922, Hoover MSS, Box 505.

4. Stover, *American Railroads*, 170–171. Serving with Harrison on the Board were Samuel Rea, Pennsylvania Railroad; Howard Elliot, New York, New Haven, and Hartford Railroad; Julius Kruttschnitt, Southern Pacific; and Hale Holden, Chicago, Burlington, and Quincy Railroad.

5. Sharfman, *The American Railroad Problem*, 79–83; Hines, *War History of American Railroads*, 13–15.

6. *Reports of the Department of Labor 1918: Report of the Secretary of Labor and Reports of Bureaus*, 117.

7. Davis, *Power at Odds*, 36.

8. Sharfman, *American Railroad Problem*, 91.

9. Kerr, *American Railroad Politics*, 14.

10. Stover, *American Railroads*, 170.

11. Kerr, *American Railroad Politics*, 63: Hines, *War History of American Railroads*, 20.

12. Stover, *American Railroads*, 173.

13. Hines, *War History of American Railroads*, 154; Kerr, *American Railroad Politics*, 92. Carter served as president of the BLFE from 1909–1922. He died in 1923.

14. "Railroad Unions United In Wage Drive," *New York Times*, November 1, 1917; "Railroad Men Want More," *New York Times*, November, 5, 1917; Hines, *War History of American Railroads*, 159; Kerr, *American Railroad Politics*, 57; "Wilson To Block Railroad Strike," *New York Times*, November 15, 1917; and "Will Not Strike, Railway Unions Assure Wilson," *New York Times*, November 16, 1917.

15. "The Truth About Wages," *Railroad Democracy*, July 29, 1919. According to figures that the paper quoted from the Bureau of Labor Statistics, 51 percent of railroad workers earned less than $75 monthly, and 80 percent earned less than $100; Hines, *War History of American Railroads*, 160.

16. Board Number 1 handled disputes from the four operating brotherhoods; Board Number 2 heard disputes from the shopcraft unions; and Board Number 3 dealt with the disputes from the clerks, telegraphers, switchmen, and maintenance of way employees.

17. Hines, *War History of American Railroads*, 169–170, 178–179.

18. Arnesen, *Brotherhoods of Color*, 42–48; Greenwald, *Women, War, and Work*, 114–115.

19. "Labor After the War," *New York Times*, November 18, 1918.

20. "Report of the Officers of the Railway Employees Department, 1920," Railroad Employees Department Collection, M. P. Catherwood Library, Labor Management Documentation Center, Cornell University, Ithaca, N.Y., Box 18 (RED Collection). These figures should be viewed with some skepticism. The most obvious weakness is that not all the RED unions' figures are reported.

21. Address of Cummins, *Iowa House of Representatives Journal*, XXXVIII, March 27, 1919, 1355–1365, quoted in Kerr, *American Railroad Politics*, 130.

22. Atlee Pomerene to Dan Dugan, August 15, 1919, Atlee Pomerene Papers, Box 1, Kent State University, Kent, Ohio (Pomerene MSS).

23. Text of President's Address to Congress, *New York Times*, December 3, 1918; Hines, *War History of American Railroads*, 43.

24. Klein, *Union Pacific*, 231.

25. Hines, *War History of American Railroads*, 43–44; Kerr, *American Railroad Politics*, 136–137; *Congressional Record*, 66th Cong., 3rd session, 1919, Vol. LVII, Part 1, 337–338; Stover, *American Railroads*, 178–179.

26. For detailed explanation of each plan, see Richard Waterman, "Proposed Plans for Railroad Legislation," in Thurman W. Van Metre, ed., *Proceedings of the Academy of Political Science in the City of New York*, VIII (January 1920): 587A–587B, William McAdoo Papers, Library of Congress, Washington D.C., Box 558 (McAdoo MSS) (Hereafter Waterman).

27. Kerr, *American Railroad Politics*, 129–130.

28. Klein, *Union Pacific*, 233.

29. Plumb and Roylance, *Industrial Democracy*, 197–199.

30. Timothy Shea to the Brotherhood of Locomotive Firemen and Engineers Board of Directors, April 18, 1919; W. S. Carter to O. W. Karn, July 24, 1920, Brotherhood of Locomotive Firemen and Engineers Collection, Labor Management Documentation Center, M. P. Catherwood Library, Cornell University, Ithaca, NY, Box 18 (BLFE Collection).

31. Keating, *Gentleman from Colorado*, 479; Olssen, "The Making of A Political Machine: The Railroad Unions Enter Politics," 387.

32. Keating, *Gentleman from Colorado*, 13–83.

33. Ibid., 478.

34. Address of Cummins, *Iowa House of Representatives Journal*, XXXVIII (March 27, 1919): 1355–1365, quoted in Kerr, *American Railroad Politics*, 143–147; Waterman, "Proposed Plans for Railroad Legislation," 587A-587B; O'Brien, *Workers' Paradox*, 85; Klein, *Union Pacific*, 235.

35. O'Brien, *Workers' Paradox*, 86; Klein, *Union Pacific*, 235.

36. Warren S. Stone, "Be Awake To Your Interests," *Brotherhood of Locomotive Engineers Journal (BLEJ)*, 54 (February 1920): 142–143. This appeared as a letter to the editor, but was apparently the text of a speech he had recently delivered in La Crosse, Wis.

37. Klein, *Union Pacific*, 235.

38. Ibid.; Waterman, "Proposed Plans For Railroad Legislation" 587A-587B; O'Brien, *Workers' Paradox*, 79–80.

39. Klein, *Union Pacific*, 238; Bryant, *History of the Atchison, Topeka & Santa Fe Railway*, 243; Daggett, *Principles of Inland Transportation*, 3rd Edition, 662–663; Zakson, "Railway Labor Legislation 1888 to 1930," 355.

40. Bryant, *History of the Atchison, Topeka & Santa Fe Railway*, 243; Daggett, *Principles of Inland Transportation*, 662–663.

41. "The Transportation Act," *BLEJ*, 54 (April 1920): 364–366; "Why We Object," *BLEJ*, 54 (April 1920): 367–368; "Arm For the Coming Battle," *Brotherhood of Locomotive Firemen and Enginemen's Magazine (BLFEM)*, 68 (April 1, 1920): 6–7.

42. "Labor to Clean House in Congress," *BLEJ*, 54 (June 1920): 540.

43. "No Party Politics," *BLEJ*, 51 (November 1917): 1029.

Chapter 4. Grassroots Political Organization

1. "No Party Politics," *BLEJ*, 51 (November 1917): 1029.

2. Warren S. Stone, "Will You Do Your Part?" *BLEJ*, 54 (June 1920): 519–520; "Labor To Clean House In Congress," *BLEJ*, 54 (June 1920): 540; "The Transportation Act of 1920," *BLEJ*, 54 (April 1920): 364–365; "Why We Object," *BLEJ*, 54 (April 1920): 367–368.

3. "The Transportation Act of 1920," *BLEJ*, 54 (April 1920): 364–365; "Why We Object," *BLEJ*, 54 (April 1920): 367–368.

4. "Minutes of a Conference between the Labor Committee of the Association of Railway Executives and the Associated Standard Recognized Railroad Labor Organizations," (Conference Minutes), 5–7, 22–25, Box 42, RED Collection; B. A.

Worthington to Daniel Willard, October 8, 1920, Northern Pacific Records Microfilm (NP), Reel 11.

5. E. E. Loomis to Daniel Willard, October 14, 1920, NP, Reel 11.

6. "A Statement of the Case for the Railway Shopmen: Rules and Contracting Out Work," Warren G. Harding Papers, Microfilm Edition, Ohio Historical Society, Columbus, Ohio, Reel 149 (Harding MSS); Daggett, *Principles of Inland Transportation*, 664.

7. W. S. Carter to O. W. Karn, July 24, 1920, BLFE Collection, Box 18; W. S. Carter to O. W. Karn, December 29, 1920, BLFE Collection, Box 18.

8. Raymond Lonergan, "Labor's Editorials and Cartoons Rile 2 Ohio Statesmen," *Labor*, April 24, 1920.

9. "The Vote Is the Thing," 54 *BLEJ*, (June 1920): 485–486; "A Call To Political Action," *BLEJ*, 54 (August 1920): 649–650; F. O. Brantly, "The Only Remedy," *BLEJ*, 54 (August 1920): 665; Samuel Gompers, Frank Morrison, and James O'Connell, "A Call to Labor For Political Cooperation," *BLEJ*, 54 (August 1920): 721–722; "Our Duty is Plain This Year," *BLEJ*, 54 (September 1920): 744; Olssen, "The Making of a Railroad Political Machine," 376–377.

10. "Gompers Would Form 50,000 Committees to Carry on Campaign," *BLEJ*, 54 (June 1920): 529–530; "'No Party' Campaign Bringing Results," *BLEJ*, 54 (July 1920): 570.

11. Edward Keating to Editors of Railroad Labor, September 10, 1924, Edward Keating Papers, University of Colorado at Boulder, University Library Archives, Box 6 (Keating MSS); Keating, Memorandum on the part played by railroad labor in senate campaigns during the last 10 years, 1922–1932, 1934, Keating MSS, Box 4; Olssen, "The Making of a Railroad Political Machine," 385.

12. Neprash, *The Brookhart Campaigns*, 32–33; McDaniel, *Smith Wildman Brookhart*, 84. The Rochdale system, which was in vogue in Great Britain, consisted of a system of cooperative stores. Wages and earnings of capital were fixed and profits were to be distributed to members. The system was to operate on a cash-only basis.

13. "Cummins Wins: But Old Guard Is Given Hard Jolt," *Labor*, June 19, 1920.

14. Donald Ramsey, "Esch of Rail Bill Fame Given Exit By Joseph Beck," *Labor*, September 18, 1920; Olssen, "The Making of a Railroad Political Machine," 381; Margulies, *The Decline of the Progressive Movement in Wisconsin*, 263.

15. Official Circular Number 125, Railroad Employees Department, American Federation of Labor, September 22, 1920, Labor Management Documentation Center, M. P. Catherwood Library, Cornell University, Ithaca, New York, Microfilm Edition, Reel 89 (RED Microfilm).

16. "Shot the Chutes For Support of Railroad Bill," *Labor*, October 2, 1920; RED Circular, No. 125, September 22, 1920, RED Microfilm, Reel 89.

17. Robert M. La Follette to William Johnston, June 28, 1920, La Follette Family Collection, Library of Congress, Washington D.C., Series B, Box 180 (La Follette MSS).

18. RED Circular Letter No. 125, RED Microfilm, Reel 89.

19. "The Labor Party," *BLEJ*, 54 (April 1920): 371.

20. Hawley, *The Great War and the Search for a Modern Order*, 57.

21. La Follette and La Follette, *Robert M. La Follette: Volume II*, 1026; "Bureau of Information on Legislative Matters Created at Conference," *Labor*, December 25, 1920.

22. L. E. Sheppard to B. M. Jewell, April 20, 1921, RED Microfilm, Reel 4.

23. W. H. Johnston to B. M. Jewell, December 9, 1921, RED Microfilm, Reel 4.

24. Ibid.

25. "Labor Plans Union of Liberal Forces: Conference Called," *Labor*, February 11, 1922.

26. MacKay, *The Progressive Movement of 1924*, 62–66.

27. "Politicians Alive To Importance of Labor Conference," *Labor*, February 18, 1922.

28. "Political Movement Launched to Rescue Government From Control of the Privileged Interests," *BLFEM*, 72 (March 15, 1922): 3–4; Clint Houston, "New Declaration of Independence Adopted By Chicago Conference," *Labor*, March 4, 1922.

29. Taft, *The A.F. of L. in the Time of Gompers*, 480.

30. See McCartin, *Labor's Great War*.

31. Link, ed., *The Papers of Woodrow Wilson, Volume 59, May 10–31, 1919*, 290–291, cited in Lichtenstein, *State of the Union*, 4–5.

32. Montgomery, "The 'New Unionism' and the Transformation of Workers' Consciousness in America, 1909–1922," 517.

33. Green, *The World of the Worker*, 93; Montgomery, "The 'New Unionism' and the Transformation of Workers' Consciousness in America, 1909–1922," 515–517; McCartin, *Labor's Great War*, 202; Dubofsky, *The State and Labor in Modern America*, 76–77.

34. "125 Arrested in Red May Day Parade Here," *Cleveland Plain-Dealer*, May 2, 1919; "Bomb Test Set for May Day," *Cleveland Press*, May 1, 1919.

35. "A Plea For Immediate Action: Statement by General W. W. Atterbury, Vice-President, Pennsylvania Railroad Company, and Chairman of the Labor Committee of the Association of Railway Executives, to the United States Railroad Labor Board, at Chicago, Monday, January 31, 1921," NP, Reel 11; Davis, *Power at Odds*, 52; Middleton, et al., *Encyclopedia of North American Railroads*, 156–157.

36. "A Plea For Immediate Action: Statement by General W. W. Atterbury, Vice-President, Pennsylvania Railroad Company, and Chairman of the Labor Commit-

tee of the Association of Railway Executives, to the United States Railroad Labor Board, at Chicago, Monday, January 31, 1921," NP, Reel 11.

37. RED Special Circular A-3, January 31, 1921, RED Microfilm, Reel 89; Jones, *Railroad Wages and Labor Relations, 1900–1952*, 69.

38. Davis, *Power at Odds*, 51; Montgomery, *Fall of the House of Labor*, 398; Hawley, *The Great War and the Search for Modern Order*, 57; Jones, *Railroad Wages and Labor Relations, 1900–1952*, 67–68.

39. Jones, *Railroad Wages and Labor Relations, 1900–1952*, 69.

40. Quote from, "Scope of Wage Reduction Extended in New Order," *Railway Age*, 71 (July 2, 1921), 13–14; Wood, *Union-Management Cooperation on the Railroads*, 75.

41. "Labor Leaders Meet in Chicago to Determine Policy on Wage Reduction," *Railway Age*, 71 (July 9, 1921): 69.

42. "Another Crisis on the Railroads," *Railway Age*, 71 (October 22, 1921): 745.

43. A. E. Lyon, "Government Regulation of Railroad Labor Relations Since 1920: United States Railroad Labor Board; United States Board of Mediation; National Mediation Board," no date, Railroad Labor Executives Association Collection, Labor Management Documentation Center, M. P. Catherwood Library, Cornell University, Ithaca, NY, (RLEA) Box 1.

44. Zieger, "From Hostility To Moderation," 27.

45. "Rail Union Leaders Order Nation-Wide Strike For October 30; 750,000 Men Quit Then On 17 Roads; 1,250,000 More To Follow; Peace Move By Harding; Food Rationing Considered Here," *New York Times*, October 16, 1921; "Railway Lines Affected by First Strike Call; Will Tie Up 97,238 Miles of Track on First Day," Ibid.

46. "President Starts Action," *New York Times*, October 16, 1921.

47. Ibid.

48. "Must Obey Board Rulings Both Unions and Road to be Held to Strict Account by Government," *New York Times*, October 19, 1921.

49. "Another Crisis on the Railroads," *Railway Age*, 71 (October 22, 1921): 745–746. While some union leaders may have personally believed in government control, there is no evidence that the standard unions were still actively trying to bring it about.

50. "Army Is Prepared to Run Big Railroads; Daugherty Hints Strike Might be Conspiracy," *New York Times*, October 25, 1921.

51. D. B. Ryland to Herbert Hoover, October 27, 1921, Hoover MSS, Commerce Papers, Box 507. There are numerous letters to Hoover opposing the strike or any government compromise on the issue.

52. United States Railroad Labor Board, Decision No. 299, October 29, 1921, NP, Reel 12.

53. Minutes of Meeting of Joint Executive Committee Held in Chicago, October 27, 1921, BLFE Collection, Box 146; Report of President and Assistant President, *BLFE Convention Proceedings, 1922*, 21–24; Jones, *Railroad Wages and Labor Relations, 1900–1952*, 71.

54. "A Fundamental Weakness of the Transportation Act," *Railway Age*, 71 (November 5, 1921): 861–862.

55. Wolf, *The Railroad Labor Board*, 330.

56. "New Rules for Shop Crafts Equivalent to Wage Cut," *Labor*, December 10, 1921; "Pensy Officials Again Defy Labor Board's Decision," *Labor*, September 10, 1921.

57. "Rail Management Defies Labor Board To Enforce Awards," *Labor*, May 13, 1922; Zieger, "From Hostility to Moderation," 27; Clint C. Houston, "AB&A Rail Strike Accepted As Test of A Common Cause," *Labor*, April 9, 1921.

58. Dubofsky, *The State and Labor in Modern America*, 92.

59. "Beck's Bill Would Put End to Dummy Contract Evasion," *Labor*, March 18, 1922.

60. Jones, *Railroad Wages and Labor Relations, 1900–1952*, 75–76.

61. William Johnston to Warren Harding, July 12, 1922, Harding MSS, Reel 149; Taft, *The A.F. of L. in the Time of Gompers*, 472. In 1923 the Supreme Court upheld the lower court's ruling. Chief Justice William Howard Taft writing for the majority stated that Congress had not granted the RLB the power to enforce its decisions; see *Pennsylvania Railroad Co. v. Railroad Labor Board*, 261 U.S. 72 (1923).

62. Davis, *Power at Odds*, 64–68. On pages 67–68 in Table 7, "Number and Percentage of Shopmen on Strike," Davis cites the percentage of striking shopmen on each carrier. According to his figures, 256,435 men went on strike.

63. "President Stands Behind Labor Board," *New York Times*, July 1, 1922.

64. Labor Board Resolution, July 3, 1922, Harding MSS, Roll 160; Dubofsky, *The State and Labor in Modern America*, 93; "Hooper 'Outlaws' Shop Craft Unions, and Draws Hot Reply from Jewell," *Labor*, July 8, 1922; Davis, *Power at Odds*, 73–74.

65. "Board 'Usurpation' Assailed by Jewell," *New York Times*, July 5, 1922.

66. Figures cited from Davis, *Power at Odds*, 71–72.

67. Ibid., 84–85; "Masked Men Beat California Shopmen," *New York Times*, July 14, 1922.

68. "Weeks Ready To Move Troops in Texas Hold States Responsible for Order; Jewell says he holds out for Justice," *New York Times*, July 14, 1922; "50 Federal Deputies To Ride Mail Trains," Ibid.; Zieger, *Republicans and Labor 1919–1929*, 129–130.

69. Ibid., 130–132; Bernstein, *The Lean Years*, 211–212; Dubofsky, *The State and Labor in Modern America*, 95.

70. Richberg, *My Hero*, 125–126; Bernstein, *The Lean Years*, 211–212.

71. Warren S. Stone, Letter to the Editor, *BLEJ*, 56 (April 1922): 241. By 1922 a regular column in the *BLEJ* was titled "The Road to Political Power."

72. "Stone's Address," *BLFEM*, 72 (June 1, 1922): 6–7.

73. "Proceedings Joint Meeting of the Legislative Boards of the ORC, BLE, BLF & E, and BRT," San Francisco, August 3, 1922, BLFE Collection, Box 170; William G. McAdoo to Daniel C. Roper, July 10, 1922, McAdoo MSS, Box 265.

74. "Prepare For The Battle of the Ballots-Immediate Action Needed," *BLFEM*, 73 (July 15, 1922): 5. Donald Ramsey, "Register, Organize, Educate, Is Trinity Needed For Victory," *Labor*, October 7, 1922.

75. "'Remember Daugherty' Is The Rallying Cry For Election Day," *Labor*, November 4, 1922; Zieger, *Republicans and Labor 1919–1929*, 142–143.

76. Donald Ramsey, "Reactionaries Routed Regardless of Partisan Label," *Labor*, November 11, 1922.

77. "The Road to Political Power," *BLEJ*, 56 (December 1922): 912; Thelen, *Robert M. La Follette and the Insurgent Spirit*, 172. The figures are from the *BLEJ*. Thelen reports slightly different figures; the GOP majority in the House shrunk from 169 to less than 20, and in the Senate from 24 to 10.

78. Ramsey, "Reactionaries Are Routed Regardless of Partisan Label," *Labor*, November 11, 1922; "American Labor Wins Most Significant Victory in Recent Election," *BLFEM*, 73 (November 15, 1922): 1–3; "The Road To Political Power," *BLEJ*, 56 (December 1922): 912–915; "The Defeat of the Old Guard," *BLEJ*, 56 (December 1922): 889.

79. Draft of Senator La Follette's New Years Message to Labor, 1922, prepared for *The American Federationist*, La Follette MSS, Series B, Box 225; Undated Memorandum, La Follette MSS, Series B, Box 195; Text of Senator Robert La Follette's Speech, November 18, 1922, La Follette MSS, Series B, Box 225; Thelen, *Robert M. La Follette and the Insurgent Spirit*, 171; Waterhouse, *The Progressive Movement of 1924 and the Development of Interest Group Liberalism*, 8.

80. "Proceedings of the Second Conference of the CPPA," 10, 28–29, in MacKay, *The Progressive Movement of 1924*, 68–70.

81. MacKay, *The Progressive Movement of 1924*, 70–71. The other planks of Keating's platform included: that Congress end the practice of the courts declaring legislation unconstitutional; increased tax rates on large income and inheritance, and payment of a soldiers' bonus by restoring the tax on excess profits; legislation providing minimum essential standards of employment for women; equality for women and men while improving existing political, social, and industrial standards; and state action to insure maximum benefit of federal maternity and infancy acts.

82. "His Only Hope," *BLEJ*, 56 (November 1922): 828.

Chapter 5. The Road to Political Power, 1922–1924

1. C. Bascom Slemp to Fred H. Fljozdal, December 31, 1923, Library of Congress, Washington, D.C., Presidential Papers of Calvin Coolidge, Microfilm edition (Coolidge MSS), Reel 39; "The President's Recent Message to Congress," *BLFEM*, 76 (January 1924): 9.

2. Zieger, *Republicans and Labor*, 158–159. The shopmen's strike of 1922 was the first national railroad strike since the Pullman strike in 1894, but nationwide strikes were threatened in 1920, 1921, and 1925.

3. "Significant Labor Developments," *Railway Age*, 77 (December 27, 1924): 1151–1152.

4. B. M. Jewell to Warren S. Stone, November 8, 1922; David B. Robertson to B. M. Jewell, November 14, 1922, RED Microfilm, Reel 4.

5. Richberg, *My Hero*, 162; Donald Richberg to B. M. Jewell, December 21, 1922, RED Collection, Box 38.

6. Donald Richberg to David B. Robertson and B. M. Jewell, February 25, 1923; in Vadney, *The Wayward Liberal*, 42; Eggert, *Railroad Labor Disputes*, 2.

7. David E. Lilienthal, "Labor and Human Problem of Railroading," RED, Box 38. This is a rough draft of an article that he submitted to labor publications.

8. Ibid.

9. "Brotherhoods Draft Railroad Labor Bill," *BLEJ*, 58 (April 1924): 265–266.

10. "The Railroad Labor Act," undated, La Follette MSS, Series B, Box 209; Memorandum of Principles and Suggestions for Proposed Legislation, RED Microfilm, Reel 1; Lilienthal, "Labor and Human Problem of Railroading," RED Collection, Box 38.

11. "David Robertson, Union Leader," *New York Times*, September 28, 1961; Fink, ed. *Biographical Dictionary of American Labor Leaders*, 307–308.

12. Dubofsky, *The State and Labor in Modern America*, 92.

13. Ibid; *Pennsylvania Railroad Company v. United States Railroad Board, et al.*, 261 U.S. 72, *Supreme Court Reporter*, (St. Paul: West Publishing Company, 1924), 260–262; "Put it to Sleep," *The American Federationist*, XXXX (August 1923): 663–665.

14. Daniel Willard to Calvin Coolidge, August 30, 1923, Coolidge MSS, Reel 38.

15. "Atterbury Flays Interference in Railroad Affairs," *Akron Beacon-Journal*, December 7, 1921.

16. Brotherhood of Railway and Steamship Clerks, Letter Number 158, March 17, 1924 and Number 159, April 1, 1924, RED Collection, Box 38; Baltimore and Ohio System Federation, Number 30-Cincinnati, March 29, 1924, RED Collection, Box 38; Senator Arthur Capper to L. C. Weeks, March 12, 1924, RED Collection,

Box 38; "Support the Railway Labor Bill," *BLEJ*, 58 (April 1924): 247; David B. Robertson to All Chief Executives, May 8, 1924, RED Collection, Box 38; E. R. Kinley to Calvin Coolidge, May 23, 1924, Coolidge MSS, Reel 39.

17. "U.S. Chamber of Commerce Opposes Howell-Barkley Bill," *Railway Age*, 77 (November 11, 1924): 963; Alfred Thom to Calvin Coolidge, September 3, 1924, Coolidge MSS, Reel 155.

18. A. C. Terry to Calvin Coolidge, January 17, 1925, Coolidge MSS, Reel 155; "Says Labor Board Has No Real Power," *New York Times*, March 30, 1924; "Railroad Officials Back labor Board," *New York Times*, March 29, 1924; "Roads Start Fight On Barclay [*sic*] Bill," *New York Times*, April 23, 1924.

19. David B. Robertson to All Chief Executives, March 20, 1924, RED Collection, Box 38; "Railroads Fight Howell-Barkley Bill," *BLEJ*, 58 (May 1924): 347; "La Follette Moves Quickly in Congress," *New York Times*, June 1, 1924.

20. "Railway Labor Bill on Floor of House of Representatives," *BLFEM*, 76 (June 1924): 293–295; "Test For House Rule on Labor Board," *New York Times*, May 5, 1924; *Congressional Record*, 68th Cong., 1st sess., 1924, Vol. 65, pt. 7, 6655.

21. "Petition Advances Labor Board Bill," *New York Times*, April 22, 1924; "House Filibuster On A Railroad Bill," *New York Times*, May 6, 1924; *Congressional Record*, 68th Cong., 1st sess., 1924. Vol. 65, pt. 8, 7874–7875.

22. *Congressional Record*, 68th Cong., 1st sess., 1924. Vol. 65, pt. 8, 7688–7876.

23. "Blocks House Bill to End Rail Board," *New York Times*, May 7, 1924.

24. David B. Robertson, William H. Johnston, E. H. Fitzgerald, and William S. Brown to All Chief Executives, February 28, 1924, RED Collection, Box 38.

25. "How They Answered the Roll Call on the Railway Act," *Railway Maintenance of Way Employees Journal*, XXXIII, (June 1924): 19–21; "Congressman Cooper of Ohio Opposes Railway Labor Bill," *BLFEM*, 77 (July 1924): 19–20.

26. "Election of Magnus Johnson of Great National Significance," *BLFEM*, 77 (July 1923): 99–101.

27. "Great Britain's Labor Government," *BLFEM*, 76 (March 1924): 110; "Labor gains in German and French Elections," *BLEJ*, 54 (June 1924): 439; Waterhouse, *The Progressive Movement of 1924 and the Development of Interest Group Liberalism*, 8–9.

28. "The Brotherhood of Locomotive Engineers Convention," *BLFEM*, 77 (August 1924): 96–98.

29. Edward Keating, "Coolidge Sure to be Nominated—Who will be Democratic Presidential Nominee?" *BLFEM*, 76 (June 1924): 295; "The Republican National Convention," *BLFEM*, 77 (July 1924): 3–7.

30. Burner, *The Politics of Provincialism*, 107–111; "McAdoo Admits Another Big Fee," *New York Times*, February 28, 1924.

31. Slayton, *Empire Statesman*, 208.

32. "State Democrats put Smith in the race for the Presidency and give him ovation: Hughes says people will keep Coolidge," *New York Times*, April 16, 1924; Burner, *The Politics of Provincialism*, 112; Slayton, *Empire Statesman*, 202–208.

33. Slayton, *Empire Statesman*, 213. According to Slayton, the convention failed by one vote to condemn the KKK by name. Slayton gives a concise, balanced account of the convention's proceedings.

34. Ibid., 214.

35. Ibid., 210–211.

36. J. H. Stapp to William G. McAdoo, June 19, 1924; Sidney Burt to William G. McAdoo, June 21, 1924; A. E. Peterman to William G. McAdoo, June 21, 1924; Memphis Brotherhood of Railway Clerks to McAdoo, July 7, 1924, McAdoo MSS, Box 306. Quote from Stapp's telegram.

37. Keating, *The Story of "Labor,"* 156.

38. Burner, *The Politics of Provincialism*, 117.

39. Ibid., 246–247.

40. Basil M. Manley to Robert La Follette, Sr., October 9, 1922, La Follette MSS, Series B, Box 95; "La Follette Ready to Run Unless Both Parties Mend Ways, Denounces Communists," *Chicago Daily Journal*, May 28, 1924, newspaper clipping in La Follette MSS, Series B, Box 207.

41. MacKay, *The Progressive Movement of 1924*, 117–120; Waterhouse, *The Progressive Movement*, 9; "The Cleveland Liberty Bell," *BLEJ*, 58 (August 1924): 571–572; Thelen, *Robert M. La Follette and the Insurgent Spirit*, 183.

42. Porter and Johnson, comps., *National Party Platforms, 1840–1968*, 252–256.

43. L. E. Sheppard, "Our Opportunity and Duty," *The Railway Conductor*, VLI (August 1924): 371–372.

44. Ben E. Chapin to Edward G. Clark, May 2, 1924, Coolidge MSS, Reel 158.

45. Edward Keating to William McAdoo, March 21, 1931, Keating MSS, Box 1.

46. Porter and Johnson, comps., *National Party Platforms, 1840–1968*, 263.

47. Ibid., 246–247, 252.

48. "Labor Day Address," La Follette MSS, Series B, Box 207; "Coolidge Says Tariff Is Workers Boon; Davis Advocates Laws Labor Is Seeking; La Follette Opens His Radio Campaign," *New York Times*, September 2, 1924.

49. Calvin Coolidge: Address to Visiting Delegation of Labor Men at the White House, Labor Day, 1924, Coolidge MSS, Reel 155.

50. Daniel Willard to Calvin Coolidge, September 2, 1924; Calvin Coolidge to Daniel Willard, September 4, 1924, Coolidge MSS, Reel 155.

51. Glad, *The History of Wisconsin*, 289; Thelen, *Robert M. La Follette and the Insurgent Spirit*, 185. It should be noted that the senator's health was poor; he died in June 1925.

52. L. J. Niemchesky to William W. Durbin, September 11, 1924; Nelson to H. L. Brunson, September 27, 1924, John Nelson Collection, Wisconsin Historical Society, Madison, Wis., Box 1 (Nelson MSS).

53. L. J. Niemchesky to N. D. Mook, October 8, 1924, Nelson MSS, Box 1; Keating, *The Story of "Labor,"* 157; MacKay, *The Progressive Movement of 1924,* 116.

54. Glad, *History of Wisconsin,* 289–290; MacKay, *The Progressive Movement of 1924,* 188–192.

55. Quotes from F. H. Fljozdal to All Members of the Maintenance of Way Organization in the State of Massachusetts, August 25, 1924, David I. Walsh Papers, Series 1, Box 3, College of the Holy Cross, Worcester, Mass. (Walsh MSS), Walsh lost the general election, but voters reelected him in 1926; "Candidates for Whom Our Members Should Vote November 4, 1924," *BLFEM,* 77 (November 1924): 330–345; "Support Cooper's Opponent in 19th Ohio, *BLFEM,* 77 (October 1924): 264; Edward Keating, "La Follette-Wheeler and a Progressive Congress, *BLFEM,* 77 (October 1924): 255; "List of Nominees for Senate and House of Representatives to be Supported in General Election, 1924," *The Railway Conductor,* LXI (November 1924): 491–493; "Give These Men Your Support," *The Railway Maintenance of Way Employees Journal,* XXXIII (November 1924): 5–8. The defeated senators were L. Heisler Ball (R-DE), Nathaniel B. Dial (D-SC), Davis Elkins, (R-WV), Medill McCormick (R-IL), John K. Shields (D-TN) and Thomas Sterling (R-SD).

56. "No Apologies," *BLEJ,* 58 (December 1924): 885.

57. Waterhouse, *The Progressive Movement of 1924 and the Development of Interest Group Liberalism,* 76.

58. Memorandum: On the Part Played by Railroad Labor in Campaigns during the Last Ten Years, 1922–1932, Keating MSS, Box 4.

59. "Prospects for the New Congress," *BLEJ,* 58 (December 1924): 886; Robert La Follette to Fred L. Holmes, Undated telegram, La Follette MSS, Series B, Box 204.

60. "Results of the Election," *Railway Age,* 77 (December 15, 1924): 898.

Chapter 6. The Railway Labor Act

1. See Hawley, *The Great War and the Search for Modern Order;* Galambos, "The Emerging Organizational Synthesis In Modern American Society."

2. David B. Robertson to Bert M. Jewell, October 14, 1924, RED Collection, Box 38.

3. L. G. Griffing and David B. Robertson to Calvin Coolidge, October 1, 1924; C. Bascom Slemp to L. G. Griffing, October 2, 1924; L. G. Griffing and David B. Robertson to C. Bascom Slemp, October 2, 1924, Coolidge MSS, Reel 39.

4. Warren S. Stone to The Chief Executives, October 24, 1924, RED Collection,

Box 38; "Rail Unions Will Press Fight on Labor Board," *New York Times*, November 8, 1924.

5. MacKay, *The Progressive Movement of 1924*, 204.

6. "Fight Organized By Executives for Howell-Barkley Bill—New Political Party Not Favored," *BLFEM*, 78 (January 1925): 11–12; Bert M. Jewell to Dorothy Gehlert, November 13, 1924, RED Collection, Box 39; La Follette and La Follette, *Robert M. La Follette: Volume II*, 1148–1165.

7. "C.P.P.A. Meeting in Chicago Feb. 21 To Act on Party Issue," *Labor*, January 10, 1925; "Railroad Labor Refuses to Abandon Non-Partisan Policies," *Labor*, February 28, 1925.

8. "Progressive Block Wins Senate Fight," *BLEJ*, 58 (February 1924): 107.

9. Bert M. Jewell to David B. Robertson, December 6, 1924, RED Collection, Box 39.

10. Murphy, "Agreement on the Railroads-The Joint Railway Conference of 1926," 825; *Congressional Record*, 68th Cong., 2d sess., 1924. Vol. 66, pt.1, 53–54; "Text of President Coolidge's Message to Congress," *New York Times*, December 4, 1924.

11. Memoranda from B. M. Jewell to Chief Executives of the Standard Labor Organizations, December 10, 1924, RED Collection, Box 39.

12. *U.S. Supreme Court Reports*, 261 U.S. 72.

13. Ibid.

14. Memoranda from B. M. Jewell to Labor Chiefs, August 19, 1924, RED Microfilm, Reel 1.

15. David B. Robertson, "The Howell-Barkley Bill," *BLFEM*, 78 (April 1925): 264; Summary of Report of Sub-Committee on Progress of the Howell-Barkley Bill, February 16, 1925, RED Collection, Box 39.

16. "Executives Define Position in New Program," *Railway Age*, 77 (November 22, 1924): 957.

17. "Tradition of Science In Labor Relations—Which?" *Railway Age*, 78 (March 14, 1925) 731–732.

18. Memorandum of Howell-Barkley Bill Progress, February 1–20, 1925, RED Collection, Box 39.

19. Ibid; Donald Richberg, "Railway Publicity Agents Poison Public Opinion," *Labor*, December 13, 1924.

20. "Executives Define Position in New Program," *Railway Age*, 77 (November 22, 1924): 957.

21. Memorandum of Conference between Secretary of Labor Davis and Robertson, Chairman of the Chief Executives' Sub-Committee in charge of the Howell-Barkley Bill, March 10, 1925, RED Microfilm, Reel 1; David B. Robertson to the Twenty Chief Executives Supporting the Howell-Barkley Bill, April 28, 1925, RED Collection, Box 39.

22. *U.S. Reports*, 267 U.S. 203; Bert M. Jewell to Owen D. Gorman, March 11, 1925, RED Collection, Box 39.

23. *U.S. Reports*, 267 U.S. 203; "P.R.R. Wins in Suit Brought by Unions," *New York Times*, March 3, 1925; "No Law to Compel 'Pensy' To Behave Rules High Court," *Labor*, March 7, 1925; "Situation Invites Industrial War, Is Opinion of Howell," *Labor*, March 14, 1925.

24. "Strike Ballot On Southern Pacific Cause For Action," *Labor*, December 6, 1924. According to the account in *Labor*, the principal southwestern carriers involved were the El Paso and Southwestern and the Arizona-Eastern. The Southern Pacific leased both properties.

25. "Proposed Railway Labor Legislation," *Railway Age*, 80 (January 16, 1926): 215–216.

26. Draft of Report for American Federation of Labor Executive Council, not dated, RED Collection, Box 43; Bert M. Jewell to David B. Robertson, May 8, 1925, RED Collection, Box 39; Murphy, "Agreement on the Railroads," 825.

27. David B. Robertson, "The Railway Labor Act," *BLFEM*, 81 (July 1926): 33. In addition to Robertson, the union representatives in the negotiations were William B. Prenter, BLE; L. E. Sheppard, ORC; and William N. Doak, BRT. Serving with Atterbury were Daniel Willard, B&O; P. E. Crowley, New York Central; C. H. Markham, Illinois Central; Hale Holden, Chicago, Burlington, and Quincy; Elisha Lee, Pennsylvania; and John G. Walber, New York Central.

28. D. B. Robertson to Members of the Associated Chief Executives Committee, August 14, 1925, RED Collection, Box 39; Memorandum of D. B. Robertson, July 27–October 13, 1925, RED Collection, Box 39. Robertson and Doak represented the unions, while Lee and Walber represented the carriers.

29. David B. Robertson to Bert Jewell and Donald Richberg, August 22, 1925; David B. Robertson, Bert M. Jewell, E. H. Fitzgerald, and William S. Brown to The Associated Chief Executives, October 24, 1925, RED Collection, Box 39.

30. David B. Robertson, Bert M. Jewell, E. H. Fitzgerald, and William S. Brown to The Associated Chief Executives, October 24, 1925: T. C. Cashen to Bert M. Jewell, December 16, 1925; T. C. Cashen to Bert M. Jewell, December 21, 1925, RED Collection, Box 39.

31. Memorandum of Robertson, July 27–October 23, 1925, RED Collection, Box 24; *Congressional Record*, 68th Cong., 1st sess., 1924, Vol. 65, pt. 7, 6387–6388.

32. David B. Robertson, Bert M. Jewell, E. H. Fitzgerald and William S. Brown to the Associated Chief Executives, October 24, 1925, RED Collection, Box 24; Memorandum of David B. Robertson, July 27–October 23, 1925, RED Collection, Box 39.

33. Memorandum of David B. Robertson, July 27–October 23, 1925, RED Col-

lection, Box 39; David B. Robertson to the Chief Executives, January 4, 1926, BLFE Collection, Box 165 (BLFE Collection); *Legislative History*, 3–4.

34. *Legislative History*, 5; T. C. Cashen to B. M. Jewell, December 21, 1925, RED Collection, Box 39.

35. David E. Lilienthal, "Labor and the Human Problems of Railroading," RED Collection, Box 38; Robertson to All Chief Executives, January 4, 1926, BLFE Collection, Box 165.

36. *Congressional Record*, 68th Cong., 1st sess., 1924, vol. 65, pt. 8, 7502; *Legislative History*, 3–17.

37. *Legislative History*, 3–17.

38. *Congressional Record*, 69th Cong., 1st sess., 1925, Vol. 67, pt. 1, 463.

39. David B. Robertson to The Chief Executives, January 4, 1926, BLFE Collection, Box 165; Robertson, "The Railway Labor Act," *BLFEM*, 81 (July 1926): 34.

40. David B. Robertson to All Chief Executives, January 18, 1926, BLFE Collection, Box 146.

41. Memorandum: The Minority Opposition to the Railroad Labor Bill, undated, BLFE Collection, Box 165.

42. House Committee on Interstate and Foreign Commerce, Railway Labor Disputes, H.R. 9463, 69th Cong., 1st sess., 1926, 7, reproduced in *Legislative History*, 53.

43. Donald Richberg to Homer Hoch, February 22, 1926, BLEF Collection, Box 165; David B. Robertson, "The Railway Labor Act," *BLFEM*, 81 (July 1926): 34–36.

44. Ibid., 37–38; Bernstein, *The Lean Years*, 216.

45. Daggett, *Principles of Inland Transportation*, 664–665; "What the Railway Labor Act Provides," Circular Letter, Number 30, March 13, 1926, RED Microfilm, Reel 1; Donald Richberg, "Richberg on the Railway Labor Act," *Labor*, January 16, 1926; Richberg, "How the Railway Labor Act will Work," *Labor*, May 22, 1926.

46. "Beyond the Railway Labor Act," *BLEJ*, 60 (June 1926): 407.

47. "The Wider Issue In Industry," *New York Times*, May 22, 1926.

48. "The Railroad Labor Bill." *New York Times*, February 23, 1926.

49. "Carrying Out the Watson-Parker Law," *Railway Age*, (May 29, 1926): 1424.

50. Ely, *Railroads & American Law*, 259.

51. "Beyond the Railway Labor Act," *BLEJ*, 60 (June 1926): 407.

Chapter 7. Strengthening the Railway Labor Act

1. Wiebe, *The Search for Modern Order, 1877–1920*, 297.

2. Statement of the Legislative Committee, Railway Labor Executives' Association Concerning the Record and Attitude of Congressman Robert Crosser Toward

Labor Legislation Considered by the 73rd Congress of the United States, Robert Crosser Papers, Ohio Historical Society, Columbus, Ohio, Box 2 (Crosser MSS).

3. *The Nation*, 123 (July 28, 1926): 68.

4. A. E. Lyon, Government Regulation of Railroad Labor Relations Since 1920: United States Railroad Labor Board; United States Board of Mediation, National Mediation Board, RLEA Collection, Box 1.

5. E. J. Manion to All Members, Railroad Labor Executives' Association, May 24, 1926, BLFE Collection, Box 165.

6. "Barkley Wins Out: 'Tricky' Ernst Soundly Walloped," *Labor*, November 6, 1926.

7. "Walsh Victorious Wires His Thanks to RR 'Boys,'" *Labor*, November 6, 1926.

8. "Butler Is Defeated: To Quit As Chairman," *New York Times*, November 3, 1926.

9. McDaniel, *Smith Wildman Brookhart*, 160–174.

10. "Labor's Political Awakening," *BLEJ*, 60 (December 1926): 885; "A Challenge to Progressive Statesmanship," *BLEJ*, 60 (December 1926): 885–886.

11. David B. Robertson to Bert M. Jewell, June 1, 1928, Donald Richberg Papers, Chicago Historical Society, Chicago, Ill., Box 6 (Richberg MSS).

12. Donald Richberg to Martin F. Ryan and J. A. Franklin, June 4, 1928, Bert M. Jewell to All Members of the Railroad Labor Executives Association, June 13, 1928, Richberg MSS, Box 6.

13. John Marrian to Donald Richberg, June 22, 1928; David B. Robertson to Donald Richberg, June 26, 1928, Richberg MSS, Box 6; Porter and Johnson, comps., *National Party Platforms, 1840–1968*, 286.

14. Ibid., 286–287.

15. Donald Richberg to Martin F. Ryan and J. A. Franklin, June 4, 1928, Richberg MSS, Box 6.

16. Bert M. Jewell to David B. Robertson, July 16, 1928; Donald Richberg to John Marrian, September 27, 1928, Richberg MSS, Box 6.

17. "Alfred E. Smith on Labor," *BLEJ*, 62 (September 1928): 669; Porter and Johnson, comps., *National Party Platforms 1840–1968*, 275; Bernstein, *The Lean Years*, 394.

18. Edward Keating, Memorandum: On the Part Played by Railroad labor in Several Campaigns During the Last Ten Years, 1922–1932, Keating MSS, Box 1.

19. Memorandum Concerning Establishment of Boards of Adjustment, BLFE Collection, Box 165; David B. Robertson to M. F. Barnett, June 4, 1926; David B. Robertson to T. C. Cashen, July 27, 1926, BLFE Collection, Box 146.

20. Memorandum, undated, Brotherhood of Railroad Trainmen Collection, Labor Management Documentation Center, M. P. Catherwood Library, Cornell

University, Ithaca, NY, Box 16 (BRT Collection); William Weiser to Bert M. Jewell, September 30, 1929, RED Collection, Box 42.

21. F. H. Knight to William A. Kiel, January 19, 1928, RED Collection, Box 42; Minutes of Fifth Annual Meeting of the International Association of General Chairmen of the Brotherhood of Railroad Trainmen, September 20, 1933, BRT Collection, Box 16; Daggett, *Principles of Inland Transportation*, 666.

22. *Legislative History*, 5–6.

23. David B. Robertson to Members, Railway Labor Executives Association, December 20, 1928, RED Microfilm, Reel 5.

24. Ibid; Donald Richberg to Bert M. Jewell, March 20, 1928, RED Microfilm, Reel 5.

25. David B. Robertson to Members, Railway Labor Executives Association, December 20, 1928, RED Microfilm, Reel 5.

26. *U.S. Reports*, 281 U.S. 555.

27. "Texas Court Says Clerks Have Right to Pick Spokesmen," *Labor*, August 27, 1927; "Sweeping Victory Scored by Clerks in Houston Court," *Labor*, April 28, 1928.

28. Bernstein, *The Lean Years*, 217–218.

29. *U.S. Reports*, 281 U.S. 548.

30. *U.S. Reports*, 281 U.S. 548; "A Blow to the Company Unions," *BLEJ*, 64 (July 1930): 494; O'Brien, *Workers' Paradox*, 144–147.

31. "A Blow To The Company Unions," *BLEJ*, 64 (July 1930): 494; George M. Harrison to All Chief Executives Standard Railroad Labor Organizations, July 27, 1931; F. H. Flojozdal to Members of the RLEA, October 13, 1931, BRT Collection, Box 16.

32. Railway Labor Executives' Association: Interim Report of Special Legislative Committee, Report of the Committee, January 25, 1934, BRT Collection, Box 16; "Shopmen To Ask For Five Day Week," *BLEJ*, 64 (October 1930): 749; McCaleb, *Brotherhood of Railroad Trainmen: With Special Interest in the Life of Alexander F. Whitney*, 161–163; "Union Leaders Meet," *BLEJ*, 65 (December 1931): 888–892; "With Railroad Labor," *BLEJ*, 65 (December 1931): 913; "Outline of Program of Railway Labor Executives' Association," *BLFEM*, 92 (March 1932): 175–183. The RLEA also wanted to limit the length of trains, full crew laws, workers' compensation, elimination of fellow servant assumption of risk doctrines from the Federal Employers Liability Act, the establishment of an adequate system of reserve to prevent unemployment and creation of unemployment offices or placement bureaus, and protection of rights and interests of employees affected by consolidation.

33. *Historical Statistics of the United States Colonial Times to 1970*, see Series

Q 235–250, 331–345, 721, and 733; Latham, *The Politics of Railroad Coordination 1933–1936*, 8; Fuess, *Joseph B. Eastman: Servant of the People*, 185.

34. Bernstein, *The Lean Years*, 314.

35. Statement in Behalf of Railway Labor Executives Association, Presentation to the President, September 22, 1932, RED Microfilm, Reel 91.

36. Latham, *The Politics of Railroad Coordination, 1933–1936*, 8; Vrooman, *Daniel Willard and the Progressive Management on the Baltimore and Ohio Railroad*, 99.

37. Moulton, *The American Transportation Problem*, 179–221, see especially graphs, 200: Fuess, *Joseph B. Eastman Servant of the People*, 186–187.

38. Memorandum Supporting Proposed Amendments to the Railway Labor Act, Not Dated, BRT Collection, Box 16. For a detailed discussion of the Emergency Transportation Act and the role of the Coordinator of Transportation, see Fuess, *Joseph B. Eastman: Servant of the People*, 199–210; and Childs, *Trucking and the Public Interest*, 124–126.

39. O. B. Colquitt to A. F. Whitney, December 9, 1933; George M. Harrison to All Chief Executives, February 2, 1934; Minutes of Fifth Annual Meeting of the International Association of General Chairmen, September 20–23, 1933, BRT Collection, Box 16.

40. Minutes of Fifth Annual Meeting of the International Association of General Chairmen, September 20–23, 1933; O. B. Colquitt to A. F. Whitney, December 14, 1933; A. F. Whitney to O. B. Colquitt, December 15, 1933, BRT Collection, Box 16.

41. A. F. Whitney to Franklin Roosevelt, March 13, 1934; Railway Labor Executives Association Interim Report of Special Legislative Committee, January 27, 1934, BRT Collection, Box 16; House Resolution 9689, 73rd Cong., 2nd sess., Crosser MSS, Box 4.

42. For comparison of the two bills see *Legislative History*, 773 & 793.

43. Quote from A. F. Whitney to C. C. Dill, June 6, 1934; for reprint of letter see *Legislative History*, 824.

44. J. A. Farquharson to A. F. Whitney, May 19, 1934, BRT Collection, Box 16.

45. 48 Stat. 1185–1197; Public Law 73–442, found in *Legislative History*, 720–736.

46. *Legislative History*, 722–727. Board 1 had jurisdiction over train service employees; Board 2, shop employees; Board 3, all other railroad operatives; Board 4, marine employees; Daggett, *Principles of Inland Transportation*, 666–667.

47. *Legislative History*, 733; Daggett, *Principles of Inland Transportation*, 667.

48. A. F. Whitney to Fred H. Fljozdal, May 25, 1934; A. F. Whitney to B. M. Jewell, May 31, 1934; J. A. Farquharson to A. F. Whitney, May 19, 1934, BRT Collection, Box 16.

49. Statement of the Legislative Committee, Railway Labor Executives Association, Concerning the Record and Attitude of Congressman Robert Crosser Toward Labor Legislation Considered by the 73rd Congress of the United States, Crosser MSS, Box 2.

Chapter 8. Railroad Retirement and Social Security

1. Character of Pension Plans: Class I Steam Roads in the United States, The Pullman Company, and the Railroad Express Agency, Inc., May 4, 1932, Robert F. Wagner Collection, Georgetown University, Washington D.C., Box 212, (Wagner MSS).

2. "Federal Retirement Insurance for Railroad Workers Now Before Congress," *BLFEM*, 92 (March 1932): 163.

3. There were two Railroad Retirement Acts, one in 1934 and a second the following year after the United States Supreme Court ruled the first unconstitutional. This chapter considers only the first, unconstitutional act because it established political and legal precedents used to frame the Social Security Act. President Roosevelt signed the second Railroad Retirement Act and the Social Security Act within days of each other in August 1935.

4. Gordon, *New Deals*, 240–279; Leotta, "Abraham Epstein and the Movement for Old Age Security," 359–377. Many of the participants in the creation of the Social Security Act wrote detailed accounts of their activities: Altmeyer, *The Formative Years of Social Security*; Brown, *An American Philosophy of Social Security*; Witte, *The Development of the Social Security Act*; and Stewart, *Social Security*. While these accounts are rich in detail, they tend to ignore the milieu in which these important events occurred.

5. Witte, *The Development of the Social Security Act*, 49–50. Labor's representatives on the Social Security Advisory Board included: William Green, president of the AFL; Paul Scharrenberg, secretary-treasurer of the California Federation of Labor; Henry Ohl Jr., president of the Wisconsin Federation of Labor; George Berry, president of the International Printing Pressmen and Assistants' Unions; and George M. Harrison, president of the Brotherhood of Railway and Steamship Clerks.

6. Leotta, "Abraham Epstein and the Movement for Old Age Security," 359–377; Brock, *Welfare, Democracy, and the New Deal*, 9–10. Brock notes the increased expenditures of state and local government during the 1920s, including $444 million on public welfare at the end of the decade, up from $119 million at the beginning.

7. Quotes from Huthmacher, *Senator Robert F. Wagner and the Rise of Urban*

Liberalism, 176–177; George M. Modlin, "Who Shall Support the Aged Worker?" *The Railroad Trainmen*, 46 (August 1929): 808.

8. Henry R. Corbett, "Retirement Insurance for Railroad Men," *BLFEM*, 93 (July 1932): 16.

9. For an early scholarly examination of the pension issue, see Hoffman, "The Problem of Poverty and Pensions in Old Age,": 182–195.

10. "More Old People, More Need for Pensions," *BLEJ*, 63 (March 1929): 188.

11. Brandes, *American Welfare Capitalism*, 104; Stewart, *Social Security*, 23.

12. *Historical Statistics of the United States Colonial Times to 1970*, Part 1, 10; "More Old People, More Need for Pensions," *BLEJ*, 63 (March 1929): 188.

13. Budd L. McKillips, "Pensions For Industry's Veterans," *The Railroad Trainmen*, 46 (September 1929): 914.

14. Lubove, *The Struggle for Social Security*, 135; McKillips, "Pensions for the Industry's Veterans," 914; Stewart, *Social Security*, 111–112.

15. Leotta, "Abraham Epstein and the Movement for Old Age Security," 360–361.

16. Ibid., 362–363. Epstein resigned from his position with the FOE in 1924 and three years later helped to found the American Association of Old Age Security, which did not have support from the FOE.

17. McKillips, "Pensions for the Industry's Veterans," 915; Derber in Braeman, Bremer, Brody, eds., *The New Deal*, 119; Stewart, *Social Security*, 112–113. State lawmakers feared that creating pensions would cause political backlash, so in most cases the burden fell on counties, which in turn created their own stringent criteria.

18. Mandell, *The Corporation as Family*, 106–107.

19. "Company Schemes Bar Older Workers," *BLEJ*, 63 (September 1929): 671; Brandes, *American Welfare Capitalism*, 106–107; "Company Pensions Fail," *BLEJ*, 67 (May 1933): 350; T. J. Bissett, "Facts Regarding Our Pension Assn.," *BLEJ*, 67 (October 1933): 653; "No Action on Pensions," *BLEJ*, 67 (February 1933): 103.

20. Stewart, *Social Security*, 126–129; Gordon, *New Deals*, 247; Classification of Pension Plans, Wagner MSS, Box, 212.

21. Brandes, *American Welfare Capitalism*, 107.

22. Modlin, "Who Shall Support the Aged Worker?" *The Railroad Trainmen* 46 (August 1929): 808; Brandes, *American Welfare Capitalism*, 107.

23. Gordon, *New Deals*, 248–249.

24. Lubove, *The Struggle for Social Security*, 126.

25. Licht, *Working for the Railroad*, 213.

26. Burgess and Kennedy, *Centennial History of the Pennsylvania Railroad Company*, 655.

27. Bryant, *History of the Atchison, Topeka & Santa Fe Railway*, 236.

28. Character of Pension Plans on Class I Steam Railroads, May 4, 1932, Wagner MSS, Box 212.

29. The BLE, BLFE, BRT, and the Brotherhood of Railroad Signalmen all offered pensions. Additionally, the BLE, BLFE, BRT, and ORC maintained a small facility for the aged and permanently and totally disabled members outside of Chicago, which began operation in 1891.

30. Latimer, *Trade Union Pensions Systems*, 39.

31. Stewart, *Social Security*, 20–21.

32. Stansell, *City of Women*, 31.

33. "A. F. of L Convention," *BLEJ*, 63 (November 1929): 824.

34. Speech Delivered by Mr. W. W. Royster at the Odd Fellows Hall, Oakland, California, November 17, 1935, BLFE Collection, Box 206 (hereafter Royster Speech). This was the only source I found that chronicled the early stages of his organization.

35. Minutes of Meetings of Railway Labor Executives Association, July 24–25, 1930, Pennsylvania Railroad Company Records, Personnel Department General Office Files, Hagley Museum and Archives, Wilmington, DE, Box 802 (PRR).

36. "Tighten Old-Age Funds," *BLEJ*, 59 (November 1925): 868.

37. "Prompt Action On Pensions," *BLEJ*, 64 (April 1930): 279; Latimer, *Trade Union Pensions Systems* 38.

38. McCoury, "A Legislative History of the Railroad Retirement Act," 18–23.

39. Quadagno, *The Transformation of Old Age Security*, 55; McCoury, "A Legislative History of the Railroad Retirement Act," 14–21.

40. Zahavi, *Workers, Managers, and Welfare Capitalism*, 136.

41. "Costs and Benefits," *BLEJ*, 66 (May 1932): 327; "No Action on Pensions," *BLEJ*, 67 (February 1933): 103; "Retirement Insurance Legislation," *BLEJ*, 67 (April 1933): 247.

42. A. F. Whitney, "Beware of Leeches," *The Railroad Trainmen*, 48 (September 1931): 611–612; BRT Office of the President, Special Circular, W-61, July 11, 1932, PRR, Box 1068.

43. See McDaniel, *Smith Wildman Brookhart*.

44. Arthur Burt to Robert F. Wagner, March 28, 1932, Wagner MSS, Box 212.

45. Examination of papers of several members of both houses of Congress during this period reveals that many requests were made by railroad employees to enact some form of retirement legislation. Collections examined included Senators: Edward Costigan, William McAdoo, George Norris, Robert Wagner, and David Walsh; and Representatives Robert Crosser and John Nelson.

46. Statement of Senator Robert F. Wagner Concerning A Bill To Provide Retirement Insurance for Railway Employees, etc., Not dated, Crosser MSS, Box 4; Gordon, *New Deals*, 240–279. Gordon argues that many business leaders ac-

quiesced on the issue of retirement pensions to ensure stability and industrial peace.

47. Statement of Senator Robert F. Wagner Concerning A Bill To Provide Retirement Insurance for Railway Employees, not dated, Crosser MSS, Box 102.

48. Henry R. Corbett, "Retirement Insurance for Railroad Men," *BLFEM*, 93 (July 1932): 16.

49. After Wagner introduced his version, Senator Hatfield introduced the RENPA bill that Keller introduced in the House.

50. "Wagner Proposes Railway Legislation," *New York Times*, March 3, 1932.

51. McCoury, "A Legislative History of the Railroad Retirement Act," 44–49.

52. David B. Robertson, "A Legislative History of the Railroad Retirement Act of 1934," *BLFEM*, 95 (June 1934): 406.

53. The financial foundation of the RENPA proposal, known as the Hatfield-Keller Bill, was unsound. The amount that both parties were required to pay into the system fluctuated. With the number of older Americans growing annually and railroad revenues shrinking, this bill was unacceptable to carriers. Opponents further argued that it would not create a large enough reserve fund, and would, therefore, be only a short-term solution.

54. McCoury, "A Legislative History Of the Railway Retirement Act," 30–34; "Pension Hearings January 11–19, 1933: Faults of S. 4646-RENPA Bill," Wagner MSS, Box 11; Alvanley Johnston, "Retirement Insurance Legislation," *BLEJ*, 67 (April 1933): 248. The *BLEJ* is unclear about who hired Brieby to testify at the hearings, but the assumption is that the carriers employed him.

55. *The Public Papers and Addresses of Franklin Delano Roosevelt Volume 1*, 121–122.

56. *Congressional Record*, 73rd Cong., 2nd sess., 1934, Vol. 78, pt. 6, 5697.

57. Ibid.

58. "Labor Executives Gratified, See Big Victory in Sight," *Labor*, May 15, 1934; "Solons Thanked By Rail Leaders: House to Act Friday," *Labor*, June 19, 1934.

59. See speech by Davis, *Congressional Record*, Vol. 68, pt. 11, 73rd Cong., 2nd sess., 11488; also, speech of O'Malley, ibid., 11708. Throughout the debate surrounding the bill, legislators often mentioned its pioneering nature.

60. *Congressional Record*, Vol. 78, pt. 11, 73rd Cong., 2nd sess., 11482–11489; "Solons Thanked By Rail Leaders; House to Act on Friday," *Labor*, June 19, 1934.

61. *Congressional Record*, Vol. 78, pt. 11, 73rd Cong., 2nd sess., 11698–11699.

62. Ibid., 12157–12161.

63. "Retirement Plan Will Pave Way For Permanent Laws," *Labor*, July 3, 1934.

64. United States Court of Appeals for the District of Columbia, October Term, 1934, No. 6355, Railroad Retirement Board, Et Al. vs. Alton Railroad Company, et.al.; "Decision Comes As Big Surprise Even To Rails' Lawyers," *Labor*,

October 30, 1934; "Rail Pension Law Invalid, Wheat Says," *Labor*, October 30, 1934.

65. *U.S. Reports*, 295 U.S. 330; "Chief Points of Majority Opinion," *New York Times*, May 7, 1935; "Rail Pensions Act Voided By Supreme Court 5 to 4; Social Programs in Peril," Ibid.

66. *U.S. Reports*, 295 U.S. 330; "Chief Points of Minority Opinion," *New York Times*, May 7, 1935. Concurring with Hughes were associate justices Louis Brandeis, Benjamin Cardozo, and Harlan Stone.

67. "Congress Passes Rail Pensions," *New York Times*, August 20, 1935.

Chapter 9. Railroad Unions and Labor Banks

1. Plumb and Roylance, *Industrial Democracy: A Plan For Its Achievement*, xvii. The authors define industrial democracy as "a system for the production and distribution of wealth that will insure equality of opportunity to all and guarantee to each the full enjoyment of the fruits of industry, by a share in the sum total of all production proportioned to his contribution thereto." Brody, *Workers in Industrial America: Essays on the Twentieth Century Struggle*, 56; McCartin, "'An American feeling': workers, managers, and the struggle over industrial democracy in the World War I era," in Lichenstein and Harris, eds. *Industrial Democracy in America*, 64–86.

2. "Money-Saving Power of Workers," *Labor*, November 22, 1924; Foster, *Wrecking the Labor Banks*, 7–8; Plumb and Roylance, *Industrial Democracy*, 243–271.

3. Wilentz, *Chants Democratic*, 39.

4. Ibid.

5. Foster, *Wrecking the Labor Banks*, 12.

6. "The Brotherhood of Locomotive Engineers Co-operative Bank," *BLEJ*, 54 (August 1920): 707; "How the Bank Started, *BLEJ*, 59 (August 1925): 577–578.

7. McCartin, "'An American feeling': workers, managers, and the struggle over industrial democracy in the World War I era," in Lichenstein and Harris, eds. *Industrial Democracy in America*, 67–86.

8. "Banking for Service to Democratize Financial System," *BLFEM*, 70 (January 1, 1921): 3.

9. von Loesch, *North-American Labor Banks in the Twenties*, 10.

10. Ibid., 13–15. The International Association of Machinists established the Mount Vernon Savings Bank in its Washington headquarters in May 1920. The union held little stock in the bank, although its president, William Johnston, was instrumental in forming the bank.

11. Voss, *The Making of American Exceptionalism*, 84.

12. "Banking for Service to Democratize Financial System," *BLFEM*, 70 (January 1, 1921): 3.

13. "Railroad Brotherhood Would Cut Out Middleman," *Idaho Leader*, July 19, 1919; Fredric C. Howe, "Labor and the Co-operative Movement," *Labor*, January 31, 1920.

14. "The All-American Farmer-Laborer Co-operative Convention: Address of Warren S. Stone," *BLEJ*, 54 (March 1920): 237–244.

15. "The All-American Farmer-Laborer Co-operative Convention: Address of Warren S. Stone," *BLEJ*, 54 (March 1920): 237–238.

16. "Birth of A Great Movement," *Labor*, February 28, 1920.

17. "How the Bank Started," *BLEJ*, 59 (August 1925): 578; "Launching of the Brotherhood of Locomotive Engineers Co-operative Bank," *BLEJ*, 54 (August 1920): 707–709. Because state regulation varied a great deal, a bank's charter was often based on expectation as to rigidity of examination. Size was generally not a factor. See *The Labor Banking Movement in the United States*, 78–80.

18. "The Brotherhood of Locomotive Engineers Co-operative National Bank of Cleveland," *BLEJ*, 54 (December 1920): 1010–1012.

19. Mills and Montgomery, *Organized Labor*, 345; "Engineers' Bank Grows At Rate of Million Monthly," *Labor*, September 9, 1921.

20. Mills and Montgomery, *Organized Labor*, 378; *The Labor Banking Movement*, 34–35.

21. *The Labor Banking Movement in the United States*, 46–47.

22. "The Brotherhood Investment Company," *BLEJ*, 57 (January 1923): 10.

23. Ibid., 10, 21. For a more complete listing of BLE assets and investments see "Warren S. Stone, Labor Leader, Dies," *New York Times*, June 13, 1925; and Foster, *Misleaders of Labor*, 9–11. In addition to its financial enterprises, the BLE owned all or part of the Brotherhood Watch Company; Scudder Furnace Company; Universal Finance Company; Sunbeam Groceries Company; Hobert-Stone Company; Pacific Empire Company; Pacific Insurance Company; Brotherhood Safe Deposit Company; Assured Thrift Agency; Assured Thrift Corporation; and Universal Mortgage Corporation. In addition, BLE officials entered various ventures and encouraged members to invest with them, a case in point being the $10 million Radio Corporation of which Stone was president.

24. See, for example, "Your Attention Brothers," *BLEJ*, 54 (October 1920): 814–815, which invites members to purchase bank stock; advertisement in *BLEJ*, 56 (April 1922): 270, announcing that stock in the Brotherhood Holding Company is for sale; "Chief's Page," *BLEJ*, 57 (January 1923): 10, where Stone encourages members to invest in the Brotherhood Investment Company.

25. Mills and Montgomery, *Organized Labor*, 345; *The Labor Banking Movement*

in the United States, 53; "Clerks Subscribe for Labor in Body; Bank Approved," *Labor*, May 20, 1922.

26. "Warren S. Stone, Labor Leader, Dies," *New York Times*, June 13, 1925.

27. Josephson, *Sidney Hillman*, 245.

28. Foster, *Misleaders of Labor*, 11; John L. Lewis, "An Inter-Union Labor Struggle," *The Nation*, 129 (March 18, 1925): 287–288. The magazine asked each man to present his side of the argument. Lewis complied with a written response, while Stone submitted a compilation of his statements on the subject, most of which were from the Coal River Collieries stockholders' newspaper, *Right-o'-Way*.

29. John W. Love, "Overwork Kills Warren Stone," *Cleveland Plain-Dealer*, June 13, 1925; Fred Charles, "Stone, Tireless Worker, Preached 'Eternal now'" Ibid.; "Stone's Body To Lie in Engineers Hall Tomorrow," *Cleveland Plain-Dealer*, June 14, 1925; "Death of Warren S. Stone Shocks the Entire Labor World," *Labor*, June 20, 1925; "Warren S. Stone, Labor Leader, Dies," *New York Times*, June 13, 1925.

30. George O. Barnhart, "Brotherhood Banking in the Pacific Northwest," *BLEJ*, 59 (August 1925): 590. "Seattle Awaits Opening of B. of L. E. Bank," *BLEJ*, (August 1925): 591; "The New South Hails the B. of L. E.," *BLEJ*, 59 (August 1925): 589; *The Labor Banking Movement*, 142.

31. Fraser, *Labor Will Rule*, 219: Josephson, *Sidney Hillman*, 247; Soule, *Sidney Hillman, Labor Statesman*, 145–146; von Loesch, *North-American Labor Banks in the Twenties*, 32; Plumb and Roylance, *Industrial Democracy*, 252–267; *The Labor Banking Movement*, 197–202.

32. *The Labor Banking Movement*, 207–213; von Loesch, *North-American Labor Banks in the Twenties*, 32.

33. Foster, *Wrecking the Labor Banks*, 25–26; Foster, *Misleaders of Labor*, 236.

34. "The Bank Welcomes Its Friends," *BLEJ*, 59 (August 1925): 574.

35. "Brotherhood Is Sued Over Deal By Bank," *New York Times*, August 11, 1927.

36. Albert F. Coyle, "The Rediscovery of Florida," *BLEJ*, 59 (November 1925): 812–813.

37. Harry J. Stuart, "Impressions of Venice," *BLEJ*, 60 (February 1926): 122.

38. "Venice," *BLEJ*, 60 (March 1926): 165.

39. William B. Prenter, "Interest in Venice," *BLEJ*, 60 (April 1926): 247.

40. Tebeau, *A History of Florida*, 385–387.

41. *Cut Loose From Banking=Unionism!*, BLFE Collection, Box 181. This is a pamphlet published by a disgruntled group of engineers who simply called themselves Progressive Members of the Brotherhood of Locomotive Engineers.

42. "The Brotherhood of Locomotive Engineers Fifth Triennial Convention Proceedings," quoted in Foster, *Misleaders of Labor*, 223.

43. "The Brotherhood of Locomotive Engineers Fifth Triennial Convention

Proceedings," quoted in Foster, *Wrecking the Labor Banks*, 27; "The Brotherhood of Locomotive Engineers Fifth Triennial Convention Proceedings," quoted in Foster, *Misleaders of Labor*, 228–235.

44. Foster, *Misleaders of Labor*, 222; "Huff, McDermand and Van Pelt to Manage Finances of Engineers," *Labor*, July 16, 1927.

45. "Engineers Adopt a Far-reaching Reorganization Plan," *Labor*, July 9, 1927.

46. "Johnston Becomes Head of BLE Affairs," *Cleveland Plain-Dealer*, July 1, 1927; "Engineers Adopt a Far-Reaching Reorganization Plan: Chief Johnston Given More Power, Assessment Levied," *Labor*, July 9, 1927; "Votes to Censure B of LE Officers," *Cleveland Plain-Dealer*, July 7, 1927.

47. "Change Setup of B of LE Bank," *Cleveland Plain-Dealer*, June 30, 1927; "Huff, McDermand, and Van Pelt to Manage Finances of Engineers," *Labor*, July 16, 1927. Huff was assistant grand chief engineer and a vice president of BLE's Boston bank; McDermand was president of the BLE's bank in Great Falls, Montana; and Van Pelt was the union's general chairman of the Kansas City Southern Railroad and president of the Pittsburg Loan and Finance Corporation, Pittsburg, Kansas. Huff and McDermand were appointed for six-year terms, and Van Pelt for three.

48. David B. Robertson to Roy Empey, April 26, 1929; H. A. Weber to Roy Empey, June 16, 1929, Roy Empey Papers, Wisconsin Historical Society, Madison, Wis., Box 1.

Bibliography

Primary Sources

American Federation of Labor, Railroad Employees Department, Labor Management Documentation Center, M. P. Catherwood Library, Cornell University, Ithaca, N.Y.

Brotherhood of Locomotive Firemen and Enginemen, Labor Management Documentation Center, M. P. Catherwood Library, Cornell University, Ithaca, N.Y.

Brotherhood of Railroad Trainmen, Labor Management Documentation Center, M. P. Catherwood Library, Cornell University, Ithaca, N.Y.

Brown, Charles P. *Brownie the Boomer: The Life of Charles P. Brown, an American Railroader.* H. Roger Grant, ed., DeKalb, Ill.: Northern Illinois Press, 1991.

Congressional Record, 1919–1935. Washington, D.C.: Government Printing Office.

Calvin Coolidge: Address to Visiting Delegation of Labor Men at the White House, Labor Day, 1924, Washington, D.C.: Republican National Committee, 1924.

Calvin Coolidge Papers, Library of Congress, Washington, D.C.

Edward Costigan Papers, University of Colorado, Boulder, Colo.

Robert Crosser Papers, Ohio Historical Society, Columbus, Ohio.

Ray Empey Papers, Wisconsin Historical Society, Madison, Wis.

Warren G. Harding Papers, Ohio Historical Society, Columbus, Ohio.

Historical Statistics of the United States Colonial Times to 1970. Washington, D.C.: Government Printing Office, 1975.

Herbert Hoover Papers, Herbert Hoover Presidential Library, West Branch, Iowa.

Edward Keating Papers, University of Colorado, Boulder, Colo.

Robert M. La Follette Papers, Library of Congress, Washington, D.C.

Legislative History of the Railway Labor Act, As Amended (1926 Through 1966). Washington, D.C.: Government Printing Office, 1974.

William G. McAdoo Papers, Library of Congress, Washington, D.C.

James O. Morris Papers, Labor Management Documentation Center, M. P. Catherwood Library, Cornell University, Ithaca, N.Y.

John M. Nelson Papers, Wisconsin Historical Society, Madison, Wis.

George Norris Papers, Library of Congress, Washington, D.C.

Northern Pacific Corporate Records, Microfilm Collection, University of Akron, Bierce Library, Akron, Ohio.

Order of Railway Conductors, Labor Management Documentation Center, M. P. Catherwood Library, Cornell University, Ithaca, N.Y.

Pennsylvania Railroad Collection, Hagley Museum, Wilmington, Del., and Pennsylvania Historical Society, Harrisburg, Pa.

Atlee Pomerene Papers, Kent State University, Kent, Ohio.

Railroad Labor Executives Association, Labor Management Documentation Center, M. P. Catherwood Library, Cornell University, Ithaca, N.Y.

Reed, J. Harvey. *Forty Years an Engineer: Thrilling Tales of the Rail*, Prescot, Wash: C. H. O'Neil, 1913.

Reports of the Department of Labor 1918: Report of the Secretary of Labor and Reports of Bureaus. Washington, D.C.: Government Printing Office, 1919.

Donald Richberg Papers, Chicago Historical Society, Chicago, Ill.

Franklin D. Roosevelt Papers, Roosevelt Presidential Library, Hyde Park, N.Y.

Franklin D. Roosevelt, *The Public Papers and Addresses of Franklin Delano Roosevelt Volume 1*. New York: Random House, 1938.

United States Supreme Court Reporter, 1922–1930. Washington, D.C.: Government Printing Office.

Robert F. Wagner Papers, Georgetown University, Washington, D.C.

David I. Walsh Papers, College of the Holy Cross, Worcester, Mass.

Secondary Sources

Akron Beacon-Journal, 1924.

Altmeyer, Arthur J. *The Formative Years of Social Security*, Madison: University of Wisconsin Press, 1966.

The American Federationist, 1919–1927.

Arneson, Eric. *Brotherhoods of Color: Black Railroad Workers and the Struggle for Equality*. Cambridge: Harvard University Press, 2002.

Barrett, James. *Work and Community in the Jungle: Chicago's Packinghouse Workers, 1894–1922*. Urbana: University of Illinois Press, 1987.

Bernstein, Irving. *The Lean Years*. Boston: Houghton Mifflin Company, 1960.

———. *Turbulent Years: A History of The American Worker, 1933–1945*. Boston: Houghton-Mifflin, 1970.

Blatz, Perry. *Democratic Miners: Work Relations in the Anthracite Coal Industry, 1875–1925*. Albany: State University of New York Press, 1994.

Braeman, John, Robert Bremner, and David Brody, eds. *The New Deal: The National Level. Vol. 1.* Columbus: The Ohio State University Press, 1975.

Brandes, Stuart D. *American Welfare Capitalism.* Chicago: University of Chicago Press, 1970.

Brock, William. *Welfare, Democracy, and the New Deal.* Cambridge: University of Cambridge Press, 1988.

Brody, David. *Workers in Industrial America: Essays on the Twentieth Century Struggle.* New York: Oxford University Press, 1980 & 1993.

Brotherhood of Locomotive Engineers Journal, 1917–1935.

Brotherhood of Locomotive Firemen and Enginemens Magazine, 1919–1935.

Brown, J. Douglas. *An American Philosophy of Social Security: Evolution and Issues.* Princeton: Princeton University Press, 1972.

Bryant, Keith L., Jr. *History of the Atchison, Topeka & Santa Fe Railway.* Lincoln: University of Nebraska, 1974.

Bucki, Cecelia. *Bridgeport's Socialist New Deal, 1915–36.* Urbana: University of Illinois Press, 2001.

Burgess, George H. and Miles C. Kennedy, *Centennial History of the Pennsylvania Railroad Company.* Philadelphia: The Pennsylvania Railroad Company, 1949.

Burner, David. *The Politics of Provincialism: The Democratic Party in Transition, 1918–1932.* New York: Alfred A. Knopf, 1968.

Childs, William R. *Trucking and the Public Interest: The Emergence of Federal Regulation, 1914–1940.* Knoxville: University of Tennessee Press, 1985.

Clements, Kendrick A. *The Presidency of Woodrow Wilson.* Lawrence: University of Kansas Press, 1992.

Cleveland Plain-Dealer, 1920–1934.

Cleveland Press, 1932–1934.

Cohen, Lizabeth. *Making A New Deal: Industrial Workers in Chicago, 1919–1939.* Cambridge: Cambridge University Press, 1995.

Commons, John R., et al., *History of Labor in the United States,* New York: Augustus M. Kelley Publishers, 1966.

Current History, 1925.

Daggett, Stuart. *Principles Of Inland Transportation.* New York: Harper and Brothers, 3rd Edition, 1941.

Davis, Colin J. *Power at Odds: The National Railroads Shopmen's Strike.* Urbana: University of Illinois Press, 1997.

Dubofsky, Melvyn. *The State and Labor in Modern America,* Chapel Hill: University of North Carolina Press, 1994.

Durand, John D. *The Labor Force in the United States, 1890–1960.* New York: Social Science Research Council, 1948.

Eagles, Charles W. *Democracy Delayed: Congressional Reapportionment and Urban-Rural Conflict in the 1920s.* Athens: The University of Georgia Press, 1990.

Eggert, Gerald G. *Railroad Labor Disputes: The Beginnings of Federal Strike Policy.* Ann Arbor: University of Michigan Press, 1967.

Ely, Jr. James W. *Railroads & American Law.* Lawrence: University of Kansas Press, 2001.

Feeding the Iron Hog. Cleveland: Brotherhood of Locomotive Engineers, 1927.

Fink, Gary M., *Biographical Dictionary of American Labor Leaders.* Westport, Conn.: Greenwood Press, 1974.

Flynn, James. "The Shopmen's Strike of 1922." Unpublished Ph.D. dissertation, University of Northern Illinois, 1994.

Foster, William Z. *Misleaders of Labor.* Chicago: Trade Union Educational League, 1927.

———. *Wrecking the Labor Banks.* Chicago: Trade Union Educational League, 1927.

Fraser, Steven. *Labor Will Rule: Sidney Hillman and the Rise of American Labor.* New York: The Free Press, 1991.

French, Chauncey Del. *Railroadman.* New York: MacMillan, 1938.

Fuess, Claude M. *Joseph B. Eastman: Servant of the People.* New York: Columbia University Press, 1952.

Galambos, Louis. "The Emerging Organizational Synthesis In Modern American History." *Business History Review* 44 (Autumn 1970), 279–290.

Glad, Paul. *The History of Wisconsin: Volume V, War, a New Era, and Depression, 1914–1940.* Madison: State Historical Society of Wisconsin, 1990.

Gordon, Colin. *New Deals: Business, Labor and Politics in America, 1920–1935.* Cambridge: Cambridge University Press, 1994.

Green, James R. *The World of the Worker: Labor In Twentieth-Century America.* Urbana: University of Illinois Press, 1998.

Greene, Julie. *Pure and Simple Politics: The American Federation of Labor and Political Activism, 1881–1917.* Cambridge: Cambridge University Press, 1998.

Greenwald, Maurine Weiner. *Women, War, and Work: The Impact of World War I on Women Workers in the United States,* Westport, Conn.: Greenwood Press, 1980.

Hawley, Ellis W. *The Great War and the Search for Modern Order: A History of the American People and Their Institutions 1917–1933.* New York: St. Martin's Press, 2nd Edition, 1992.

Hines, Walker D. *War History of American Railroads.* New Haven: Yale University Press, 1928.

Hoffman, Frederick L. "The Problem of Poverty and Pensions in Old Age," *American Journal of Sociology,* 14 (September 1908): 182–195.

Huthmacher, J. Joseph. *Senator Robert F. Wagner and the Rise of Urban Liberalism.* New York: Antheneum, 1968.

Idaho Leader, 1919.

Jensen, Kimberly. *Mobilizing Minerva: American Women in the First World War*, Urbana: University of Illinois Press, 2008.

Jones, Harry E. *Railroad Wages and Labor Relations, 1900–1952: An Historical Survey and Summary of Results*. New York: Bureau of Information of Eastern Railways, 1953.

Josephson, Matthew. *Sidney Hillman: Statesman of American Labor*. Garden City, N.Y.: Doubleday and Company, 1952.

Keating, Edward. *The Story of "Labor," Thirty-three Years of Rail Workers Fighting Front*. Washington, D.C.: Rufus H. Darby Printing Co., 1953.

———. *The Gentleman from Colorado*. Denver: Sage Co., 1964.

Kerr, K. Austin. *American Railroad Politics, 1914–1920: Rates, Wages, and Efficiency*. Pittsburgh: University of Pittsburgh Press, 1968.

Keyserling, Leon H. "The Wagner Act: Its Origin and Current Significance," *George Washington Law Review*, 29 (December 1960): 199–233.

Klein, Maury. *Union Pacific: The Rebirth 1894–1969*. New York: Doubleday, 1989.

Kolko, Gabriel. *The Triumph of Conservatism: A Reinterpretation of American History, 1900–1916*. New York: Free Press of Glencoe, 1963.

Labor, 1919–1934.

Labor and Banking Finance Since 1920. Washington, D.C.: Editorial Research Reports, 1927.

The Labor Banking Movement in the United States. Princeton: Princeton University Press, 1927.

La Follette, Belle C. and Fola. *Robert M. La Follette: Volume II*. New York: MacMillan Company, 1953.

Latham, Earl. *The Politics of Railroad Coordination, 1933–1936*. Cambridge: Harvard University, 1959.

Latimer, Murray Webb. *Trade Union Pensions Systems and Other Superannuation and Permanent and Total Disability Benefits in the United States and Canada*. New York: Industrial Relations Counselors, Inc., 1932.

Lecht, Leonard A. *Experience Under Railway Legislation*. New York: Columbia University Press, 1955; AMS Edition, 1968.

Leotta, Louis. "Abraham Epstein and the Movement for Old Age Security." *Labor History* 16 (Summer 1975), 359–377.

Licht, Walter. *Working for the Railroad: The Organization of work in the Nineteenth Century*. Princeton: Princeton University Press, 1983.

Lichtenstein, Nelson. *State of the Union: A Century of American Labor*. Princeton: Princeton University Press, 2002.

Lichtenstein, Nelson and Howell John Harris, eds. *Industrial Democracy in America: The Ambiguous Promise*. Cambridge: Cambridge University Press, 1993.

Lubove, Roy. *The Struggle for Social Security, 1900–1935*. Cambridge: Harvard University Press, 1968.

Luthin, Reinhard H. "Smith Wildman Brookhart of Iowa Insurgent Agrarian Politician." *Agricultural History* XXV (October 1951), 187–197.

MacKay, Kenneth Campbell. *The Progressive Movement of 1924*. New York: Octagon Books, 1972. Originally published New York: Columbia University Press, 1947.

Mandell, Nikki. *The Corporation as Family: The Gendering of Corporate Welfare, 1890–1930*. Chapel Hill: University of North Carolina Press, 2002.

Margulies, Herbert F. *The Decline of the Progressive Movement in Wisconsin 1890–1920*. Madison: The State Historical Society of Wisconsin, 1968.

Maynard, Carl E. "The Political Views of Warren G. Harding As Indicated by the Editorials of *The Marion Star* from 1906 Through 1914." Unpublished Master's Thesis, Bowling Green State University, 1951.

McCaleb, Walter F. *Brotherhood of Railroad Trainmen: With Special Reference to the Life of Alexander F. Whitney*. New York: Albert and Charles Boni, 1936.

McCartin, Joseph A. *Labor's Great War: The Struggle for Industrial Democracy and the Origins of Modern American Labor Relations, 1912–1921*. Chapel Hill: University of North Carolina Press, 1997.

McCoury, Phillip D. "A Legislative History of the Railroad Retirement Act." Unpublished Master's Thesis, Duke University, 1950.

McDaniel, George W. *Smith Wildman Brookhart: Iowa's Renegade Republican*. Ames: Iowa State University Press, 1995.

Middleton, William D., George M. Smerk, and Robert L. Diehl, eds. *Encyclopedia of North American Railroads*. Bloomington: University of Indiana Press, 2007.

Mills, Harry A. and Royal E. Montgomery. *Organized Labor*. New York: McGraw-Hill Co., 1945.

Mink, Gwendolyn. *Old Labor and New Immigrants in American Political Development: Union, Party and State, 1875–1920*. Ithaca: Cornell University Press, 1990.

Montgomery, David. *The Fall of the House of Labor: The Workplace, the State, and American Labor Activism, 1865–1925*. Cambridge: Cambridge University Press, 1987.

———. "The 'New Unionism' and the Transformation of Workers' Consciousness in America, 1909–1922." *Journal of Social History*, 7 (1974): 509–529.

Moulton, Harold G. *The American Transportation Problem*. Washington, D.C.: The Brookings Institution, 1933.

Murphy, Frank J. "Agreement on the Railroads-The Joint Railway Conference of 1926." *Labor Law Journal* 11 (September 1960), 823–835.

Nash, Gerald D. "Franklin D. Roosevelt and Labor the World War I Origins of Early New Deal Policy," *Labor History*, 1 (1960): 39–52.

The Nation, 1919–1934.

Neprash, Jerry Alvin. *The Brookhart Campaigns in Iowa 1920–1926: A Study in the Motivation of Political Attitudes.* New York: AMS Press, 1968. Originally published New York: Columbia University Press, 1932.

New York Times, 1919–1935.

Norwood, Stephen. *Labor's Flaming Youth: Telephone Operators & Worker Militancy, 1878–1923.* Urbana: University of Illinois Press, 1991.

O'Brien, Ruth. *Workers' Paradox: The Republican Origins of the New Deal Labor Policy, 1886–1935.* Chapel Hill: University of North Carolina Press, 1998.

Olssen, Erik. "The Making of a Political Machine: The Railroad Unions Enter Politics." *Labor History* 19 (Winter 1979), 373–396.

Plumb, Glenn E. and William G. Roylance. *Industrial Democracy: A Plan For Its Achievement,* New York: B. W. Huebsch, Inc., 1923.

"Poorhouses: 'The Shame of the States,'" *The American Labor Legislation Review.* 16 (September 1926), 244–245.

Porter, Kirk H. and Donald Bruce Johnson, comps. *National Party Platforms, 1840–1968.* Urbana: University of Illinois Press, 1970.

Proceedings of the Academy of Political Science in the City of New York, January 1920.

Quadagno, Jill. *The Transformation of Old Age Security.* Chicago: The University of Chicago Press, 1988.

Railroad Democracy, 1919.

Railroad Trainmen, 1921–1929.

Railway Age, 1919–1934.

Railway Conductor, 1922–1928.

Railway Maintenance of Way Employees Journal, 1922–1928.

Rayback, Joseph G. *A History of American Labor.* New York: Free Press, 1966.

Richardson, Reed C. *The Locomotive Engineer, 1863–1963: A Century of Railway Relations and Work Rules.* Ann Arbor: University of Michigan Press, 1963.

Richberg, Donald R. *My Hero: The Indiscreet Memoirs of an Eventful but Unheroic Life,* New York: G. P. Putnam's Sons, 1954.

Robbins, Edwin C. *Railway Conductors: A Study in Organized Labor.* New York: AMS Press, 1970. Reprinted by Permission of Columbia University Press, 1914.

Schatz, Ronald. *The Electrical Workers: A History of Labor at General Electric and Westinghouse, 1923–1960.* Urbana: University of Illinois Press, 1983.

Seidman, Joel. *The Brotherhood of Railroad Trainmen: The Internal Life of a National Union.* New York: John Wiley and Sons, Inc., 1962.

Shapiro, Stanley. "'Hand and Brain': The Farmer-Labor Party of 1920." *Labor History,* 25 or 26 (1985), 405–422.

———."The Great War and Reform: Liberals and labor, 1917–1919." *Labor History* Vol. 12, (1971), 323–344.

Sharfman, I. Leo. *The American Railroad Problem: A Study of War and Reconstruction*. New York: The Century Company, 1921.

Shepherd, Allen LaVerne. "Federal Railway Labor Policy, 1913–1926." Unpublished Ph.D. dissertation, University of Nebraska, 1972.

Slayton, Robert A. *Empire Statesman: The Rise and Redemption of Al Smith*. New York: Free Press, 2001.

Soule, George. *Sidney Hillman, Labor Statesman*. New York: Macmillan, 1939.

Stansell, Christine. *City of Women*. Urbana: University of Illinois Press, 1987.

Stewart, Maxwell S. *Social Security*. New York: W. W. Norton & Co., Inc., 1937.

Stover, John F. *American Railroads*. Chicago: University of Chicago Press, 1997 (Second Edition).

———. *The Life and Decline of American Railroads*. New York: Oxford University Press, 1970.

Stromquist, Sheldon. *Generation of Boomers: The Pattern of Railroad Labor Conflict in Nineteenth-Century America*. Urbana: University of Illinois Press, 1993.

Taft, Philip. *The A.F. of L. in the Time of Gompers*. New York: Harper and Row, 1957.

Tebeau, Charlton W. *A History of Florida*. Coral Gables: University of Miami Press, 1971.

Thelen, David P. *Robert M. La Follette and the Insurgent Spirit*. Boston: Little, Brown and Company, 1976.

U.S. Supreme Court Reports, Pennsylvania Railroad Co. v. United States Railroad Board, et al. 261 U.S. 72 (1923).

Vadney, Thomas. *The Wayward Liberal: A Political Biography of Donald Richberg*. Lexington: University of Kentucky Press, 1970.

Valelly, Richard M. *Radicalism in the States: The Minnesota Farmer-Labor Party and the American Political Economy*. Chicago: University of Chicago Press, 1989.

von Loesch, Achim. *North-American Labor Banks in the Twenties*. Cologne, Germany: Bank fur Gemeinwirschaft Aktiengesellschaft, 1974.

Voss, Kim. *The Making of American Exceptionalism: The Knights of Labor and Class Formation in the Nineteenth Century*. Ithaca: Cornell University Press, 1993.

Vrooman, David M. *Daniel Willard and Progressive Management on the Baltimore and Ohio Railroad*. Columbus: The Ohio University Press, 1991.

Waterhouse, David L. *The Progressive Movement of 1924 and the Development of Interest Group Liberalism*. New York: Garland Publishing, 1991.

White, William Thomas. "A History of Railroad Workers in the Pacific Northwest, 1883–1934." Unpublished Ph.D. dissertation, University of Washington, 1981.

Wiebe, Robert H. *The Search for Order, 1877–1920*. New York: Hill and Wang, 1967.

Wilentz, Sean. *Chants Democratic: New York City and the Rise of the American Working Class, 1788–1850*. New York: Oxford University Press, 2004.

Witte, Edwin E. *The Development of the Social Security Act*. Madison: University of Wisconsin Press, 1962.

Wolf, Harry D. *The Railroad Labor Board*. Chicago: University of Chicago Press, 1927.

Wood, Louis A. *Union-Management Cooperation on the Railroads*. New Haven: Yale University Press, 1931.

Zahavi, Gerald. *Workers, Managers, and Welfare Capitalism*. Urbana: University of Illinois Press, 1988.

Zakson, Lawrence Scott. "Railway Labor Legislation 1888 to 1930: A Legal History of Congressional Railway Labor Relations Policy." *Rutgers Law Journal* 20 (Winter 1989), 317–391.

Zieger, Robert H. "From Hostility to Moderation: Railroad Labor Policy in the 1920s." *Labor History* Vol. 9 (Winter 1968), 23–38.

———. *Republicans and Labor 1919–1929*. Lexington: University of Kentucky Press, 1969.

———. "Senator George Wharton Pepper and Labor Issues In the 1920s." *Labor History* Vol. 9 (Spring 1968), 163–183.

Index

Jon R. Huibregtse is associate professor and chair of the history department at Framingham State College. He lives in Westborough, Massachusetts, with his family.